THE MODERN ALCHEMIST

"Two fish swim in our sea"

THE MODERN ALCHEMIST

A Guide to Personal Transformation

by Richard and Iona Miller

11-28-12

*Complete with seventeen engravings
from* The Book of Lambsprinck
*depicting the alchemical process,
faithfully and rigorously reproduced*

by Joel Radcliffe

OAK PUBLISHING

Artist's Dedication

For their understanding, support, and patience, this
work is dedicated to my father, John,
and to my mother, Amy.

98 97 96 95 94   5 4 3 2 1

Library of Congress Cataloging-in-Publication Data

Miller, Richard Alan, 1944-
     The modern alchemist : a guide to personal transformation / by
Richard and Iona Miller.
         p.   cm.
     Includes bibliographical references and index.
     ISBN 0-933999-37-2 (pbk. : alk. paper) : $14.95
     1. Spiritual life.   2. Alchemy--Religious aspects.   3. Jung, C. G.
(Carl Gustav), 1875-1961.   I. Miller, Iona.   II. Title.
BL624.M476   1994
158'.1--dc20
                                                                    94-10217
                                                                    CIP

Printed and bound in the United States of America by Ken's Printing

Contents

Foreword 9

Introduction: Images of the Soul and Spirit 11

Part I
Metamorphosis of Soul:
Therapy or Personal Growth

Chapter 1: The Prima Materia 23
(*Persona*) "Two fish swim in our sea."

Chapter 2: The Nigredo 35
(*Shadow*) "A cruel black dragon lurks in the wood."

Chapter 3: The Union of Opposites 45
(*Anima*) "A stag and unicorn in the forest go."

Chapter 4: Participation Mystique 55
(*Animus*) "A male and female stand hidden in darkness."

Chapter 5: Solutio 63
(*The Adversary*) "The wolf and dog are in the land."

Chapter 6: Coagulatio 65
(*Great Mother*) "A poisonous dragon inhabits the forest."

Chapter 7: Sublimatio 87
(*Wise Old Man*) "Two birds lie within the nest."

Chapter 8: Albedo, Rubedo, and Coniunctio 97
(Marriage of Opposites) "A white and red bird are bound together."

Part II
Personification of Spirit:
Spiritual Development

Chapter 9: Solificatio 117
(*Hero*) "The Lord of the Forest takes his Kingdom's Throne."

Chapter 10: The Philosopher's Stone 133
(*Mana Personality*) "The Salamander comes from the fire."

Chapter 11: Puer/Senex 147
(*Magical Child*) "Father, Son, and Guide hold each other's hand."

Chapter 12: The Transcendent Function 161
(*Self or God-Image*) "The Son speaks to his Guide."

Chapter 13: Devouring Father 175
(*Conception*) "The Father swallows up the Son."

Chapter 14: Anima Consciousness 185
(*Incubation*) "The Father strongly sweats and glows."

Chapter 15: Individuation and Rebirth 201
(*Rebirth*) "The new Father brings forth a new Son."

Chapter 16: Ultima Materia 211
(*The Master or God-Man*) "The completion of the Great Work."

Appendix: A Note on *The Book of Lambsprinck*.....................213

Bibliography 215

Index 217

Foreword

IN our modern culture, traditional religion has not been able to meet the spiritual needs of many individuals. Still, these seekers yearn for a greater understanding of self and the Higher Power, however one conceives that force. To fill that gap many forms of sacred psychology have arisen. Some of these are based in the ancient mystic arts, while others have emerged from the work of psychologists like Carl Jung, who first introduced notions of transpersonal forces into his field.

Jung came upon his theories of the psyche through firsthand observation of his clients. He shared an interest in their hopes, dreams, problems, belief systems, and the myths that gave their lives meaning. He noted that religion failed to provide a guiding myth for some individuals. Nevertheless, they could look directly within, without the mediation of priests or other go-betweens and find direct experience of their soul and spirit through the process Jung termed *individuation.* Through this technique, even someone with an orthodox religious foundation could find a more intimate connection with the guiding and nurturing powers of the universe.

The direct experience of the sacred dimensions of life yields many positive results both for the personality and the spirit. First and foremost, it reunites us with alienated or "lost" parts of ourselves and allows us to find greater fulfillment. The path of individuation is a process of "coming to wholeness." Through it we can actualize our birthright, each in our own unique way. Saint Paul referred to a variation on this theme when he proclaimed, "It is sown a natural body; it is raised a spiritual body."

Depth psychology provides a great deal of insight concerning human spiritual or mystical experience. It deals most fully with the individual who may be characterized as a "seeker." Alchemy and magic were some of the psychological languages of the past. They were means for realizing the quest, or journey into the depths of the subconscious. Today, the explanations of depth psychology reveal the value of the old practices and allow us to improve our own self-awareness by drawing from its resources. Psychology provides a technical language that helps us formulate contemporary definitions for spiritual experiences that have long been referred to as "the mysteries."

Alchemy is a projection of a cosmic and spiritual drama in laboratory terms. It aims not only at rescuing the human soul, but ennobling the material basis of the cosmos. In more modern terms, it helps us ground the spirituality of an abstract, ideal state in our daily lives. Through this process we find an inner healing that includes a reconciliation of the mind/body split fostered in our culture by the rational-mechanical scientific models of the past few centuries. The total experience of being helps us transform an abstract ideal into a fully human mode of existence. Body, mind, and spirit are no longer experienced as separate. In the new paradigm of wholeness the split is healed so the human soul can find integration.

Jung spent the better part of his life studying the subject of alchemy. In typical "Jungian" style, his interest in alchemy developed from a vivid dream. Jung was amazed to find that the images and operations he encountered in the old alchemy texts related strongly to his theories of psychoanalysis and the unconscious. Therefore, his main research project at the culmination of his career concerned alchemy and its relationship to the process of consciousness.

This transformative process happens to all of us during the course of our lives. For most, it remains unconscious and takes place largely in dreams. Others seek to become consciously aware of it and facilitate its unfolding, thereby adding a sacred dimension to life that is fulfilling and rewarding on a deep level. This work leads to a worldview which unifies spirit and matter. It combines contemporary knowledge of the physical nature of the universe with psychological and spiritual understanding to yield wisdom.

Introduction

Images of the Soul and Spirit

T HE BOOK OF LAMBSPRINCK is a sixteenth-century alchemical text written by a German mystic whose name was Lambsprinck. His work shows that his orientation toward God and the universe was that of a Christian kabbalist. The Kabbalah was originally a Jewish mystical system of self-development. However, in medieval times the faiths of the pagan, Christian, and Jew melded with Greek and Egyptian philosophical thought in Hermetic philosophy. Through this system of active aspiration, the mystic sought union with his own higher aspects and God.

Why is Lambsprinck's process, with its intriguing pictorial series, relevant for us today in our modern world? Because the same processes which motivated this manuscript are still active in each of us, although we may not be consciously aware of them. This book is a description in alchemical terms of the process of psychological transformation.

This process was shown by C. G. Jung to be analogous to the process of individuation or coming-to-wholeness, experienced by many modern individuals. Hermetic philosophy is the common ground between alchemy and depth psychology. It is a means of acquiring a working relationship with the dynamic forces of the subconscious and the divine process represented by the Self.

According to Jung, we do not need to enter therapy to begin the process of inner transformation. Basic changes, phases of life experience, or crises may precipitate radical psychological change. How we relate consciously to these changes determines whether they will be for the better or worse.

We begin to wonder what is really happening to us and seek answers within, perhaps through examining our dreams or fantasies. If we are lucky enough to be transforming to a greater degree of mental health and spiritual maturity we may experience a psychological rebirth. This is a natural process that leads us toward our own unique perfection.

How does psychology define this inner dynamic which guides the process of individuation, leading toward the goal of wholeness? In Jungian psychology, this symbol-forming power of the psyche is called the *transcendent function*. Before the transforming power of the higher Self is perceived in imagination (personified through one's Angel, Guide, or Guru), it is known as a symbol-forming function. Its purpose is to mediate between that which is unknown and that which is manifest. It performs its function by creating unifying symbols from pairs of opposites. In this manner, it gradually unites the fragments of psychic life. It creates a series of symbols that transfers consciousness to a higher perspective or awareness by reconciling opposites.

By synthesizing pairs of opposites into a symbol, the transcendent mode creates a method of transition from one set of attitudes to the next. An individual ego may work more effectively with subconscious processes by consciously attaching value to these symbols presented by the transcendent function.

Our task is to discover these transpersonal meanings, whether they are presented to us through dreams, attitudes, or behavior patterns. If the meaning were consciously understood, it would not be presented as a symbol. Therefore, once its meaning is realized over a period of time, another symbol appears to take its place, reflecting the new situation.

The transcendent function—seen as one's Inner Guide, Angel, or Guru—embodies the transmuting power of the symbol. The personification of the higher Self allows us to take up a relationship with the inner Self, and encourages dialogue and the development of feelings of loving devotion for this inner friend.

All the symbols and archetypal figures in which the transformative process is embodied are vehicles of the transcendent function. It is the union of different pairs of psychological opposites (like male/female, good/evil, Sol/Luna) in a synthesis that transcends them both.

The uniting symbol only appears when the inner psychic life is experienced as just as valid, effective, and psychologically "real" as the world of daily life. Fantasy animates both our inner and outer "realities." This is why mystics call time, space, and ego the three great illusions.

The transcendent function, or Inner Guide, restores the balance between the ego and the unconscious. It belongs to neither, yet possesses access to each. It allows the soul to ascend by bridging between and participating in both inner and outer life. By relating to each independently, it unites ego and the unconscious.

The first glimmerings of "Knowledge and Conversation with one's Angel" are very similar to the descriptions of "peak experience" developed by Abraham Maslow. A peak experience is the result of the drive of the spirit in search of itself. The experience is self-validating, self-justifying, and has unique intrinsic value for each individual.

There is an intense experience of the nearness of God or divinity. This is the first state of grace, or mind-expansion. It is a response to the experience of heightened awareness of a greater Presence. The true mystic takes this experience as his point-of-departure and grows in grace from it. The poet or artist uses this recurrent experience as a basis for artistic creation, inspiration, and personal euphoria. When the contact is stabilized, the Guide can take the soul up to the heights of mystic rapture. A by-product of this contact is that the adept may consult at will with his guide for directions in any matter. This contact is known in Eastern systems as "getting the radiant form of the Master." It occurs only after one penetrates the lower astral plane, or experiential realm of imagination, through meditation.

Images of the Self appear spontaneously throughout the entire transformative process. It appears in all symbols from the highest to the lowest. At the beginning of the great work it appears in animal forms such as snakes, birds, fish, horses, or beetles. It shows through the plant forms of flowers and tree symbolism. The symbols of the Self in human forms may be contaminated with other archetypes, since pure forms are rarely seen outside of mystical meditation. For example, if one's image of the Self were contaminated with the anima/animus, the vision would be of a vibrant solar woman whose aura radiates like the sun. Contaminated by the shadow, one might experience a magical creature like Faust's Mephistopheles. When one is able to perceive the radiant form, one sees the archetype of the Self in its pure form, uncontaminated by the personal complexes that diminish its refulgence.

You may be wondering by now where alchemy comes into this process, and what the value of harking back to a seemingly medieval system of psychology may be. Alchemy, as a transcendental search or quest, sought the redemption of the soul of matter, and its subsequent reunification with spirit. Alchemy sought to redeem the corruptness of the physical body by finding divinity within it. Alchemists projected their own individual process of psychic transformation into a pseudochemical process in their retort vessel.

Alchemy actually sought to establish harmony between the voluntary action of man and the involuntary action of nature. In other words, alchemists sought unification of conscious and subconscious processes, through a spiritual redemption of the physical body. This is especially true of Christian alchemists, since the body was considered inherently evil. One solution is to visualize the physical as a metaphor for psychic transformation.

The imagery of alchemy is valuable since it concretizes and characterizes any personal experience of the unconscious. In other words, any process of psychic transformation, whether through psychotherapy or natural transformation, may be described through the metaphors of alchemical process that relate to specific stages of development.

The operations of alchemy describe induction into consciousness from the original undifferentiated state, termed the *prima materia*. Rigid aspects of the ego or personality are broken down and remolded in the image of the Philosopher's Stone through such operations as *calcinatio, solutio, sublimatio, coagulatio, circulatio,* and *coniunctio*. The number and order of these operations may vary, but the gist of the process is consistent in various writings.

In this version of *The Book of Lambsprinck*, key words from the original text are elaborated using current concepts from Jungian psychology. The stages of the alchemical process are correlated with psychological states of awareness and experience. Various phases of the alchemical *Magnum Opus*, or Great Work, are described in every-day psychological language. The pervading motif of *The Book of Lambsprinck*, reconciliation of the father and son, is dealt with in psychological terms of the *puer/senex* complex. It is the motivating archetype behind this alchemical presentation.

The Book of Lambsprinck provides a paradigm through which we may experience a restoration of the alchemical philosophy. This is possible when we are able to see the process repeating itself in the lives of individuals on a daily level in our moods and personal reactions, such as dreams and habitual behavior. This alchemical and psychological process provides a basis for unification of vision among matter, soul, and spirit.

There is value in a revival of *The Book of Lambsprinck*, since it has an eternal or immortal quality. As presented, it provides a model of applied philosophy, relevant to the contemporary spiritual quest. It outlines a psychology of religious endeavor. It proves insight for students of philosophy, psychology, and metaphysics.

The prints may be used as focal points for meditation during the various stages you may find yourself experiencing. As symbolic images, these prints exert an active influence on the subconscious. Visual contact with them stimulates the process they represent. In other words, they evoke subconscious forces into dynamic, conscious activity. They might be used as starting points for creative imagination. They provide a guiding path for the journey into the subconscious.

Despite the interesting overlap in paradigmatic approaches, there is a crisp distinction between the world views of psychotherapy and spiritual discipline. What is considered meaningful and what is regarded as trivial depends on which archetype is most strongly activated in your own psyche.

Though it speaks frequently of soul and soul-making, psychology may regard spiritual discipline as a transcendent fantasy or escapism. On the other hand, one's spiritual teacher might regard analysis as a waste of time spent concentrating on illusions rather than lofty absolutes. We can derive benefit from both schools of thought if we maintain a metaphorical approach to both, since both may seem "as if" they are "real." Certainly we can find meaningful guidance from both. We need to find connections between spirit's upward drive and matter's encumbering embrace. This was the alchemist's path to liberation.

The original engravings that accompanied the text have been beautifully rendered into pen-and-ink drawings by Seattle artist Joel Radcliffe. Though these images have appeared in numerous sources, they have been photographic reproductions of the engravings, poorly reproduced and lacking aesthetic appeal. The laborious seven-year process of refining the plates tempered Radcliffe's soul, and he remained faithful to the style and content of the originals. We hope you enjoy them, as we have.

LAMBSPRINCK'S INTRODUCTION

My name is Lambsprinck, born of a free people.
I am entitled to carry this coat of arms by right and with glory.

I have understood pure wisdom;
Through art I have penetrated to the root of everything.

And God's grace has granted me
Wisdom together with Understanding.

For this reason am I Author of this Book,
Revealing something that is truly worthwhile,
So Rich and Poor may understand it.

What I have to disclose has no equal on Earth;
Something that I have studied deeply,
While examining the foundation of truth.

You will also find this Book is true,
If you read it often and heed its contents.

In this way you will come to learn Wisdom,
Making the best use of this gift that God grants you.

O God! Who is both end and beginning,
We beg you through Jesus Christ,
To guide our intellectual purpose,
So that we may thank you with unreserved praise!
Desiring only to perfect your will on Earth,
Using this book and all your creatures only for good.

Establish us in Charity,
Born of the Holy Trinity.

Now with God's help I will begin,
Keeping nothing back.

If you understand me correctly,
You will return from Error.

There is only *one* substance,
In which all others are concealed.

Do not let this discourage you;
Time must test your patience.

You must *will* to seize the noble fruit!
Do not be put off by time and hard work.
For you must ripen the seed of the metals,
Day by day over the weeks.

Thus you will discover
And perfect the whole art of this pure wisdom.

Something the whole world believed impossible,
Though convenient and easy.

We cannot publish it openly,
Or all men would laugh at us.

For this reason remain silent and live in obscurity,
So you may live in peace without trouble,
Keeping a pure reputation before God and all men.

Thus is the Art kept secret.

Now I shall end my Introduction
And begin to describe the Art
In words and pictures
So the light may quite clearly shine.

Thanking the Creator of all things,
The first picture follows.

PART I

Therapy or Personal Growth

"Two fish swim in our sea"

PLATE 1

The Wise say in accord
That *two fish swim in our sea;*

Neither of them have flesh or bones.
Let them achieve maturity in their own water;
Then they too will become a great sea,
The vastness of which no man can describe.

Such is argent refined red lead.

There are two fish yet there was one;
They are both equally important, and yet they are both one.

Every material object is composed of three things:
Matter (*Corpus*), Spirit (*Spiritus*) and Soul (*Anima*).

Now I tell you further that these three should be united,
So that they are all assimilated in the great sea.
A similar process can take place within yourselves,
And you should have great powers of growth.

Thus Sulphur rightly evolves by the action of Sulphur,
And in this way no weakness ensues.

Acquire discretion to your great advantage,
So that you may lose all poverty of Spirit.

Guard your tongue:
Advance your affairs unknown to any man.

You should understand and note
That *two fish swim in our sea.*

The sea is Matter and the two fishes are Soul and Spirit.

Chapter 1: Persona

The Prima Materia

ALCHEMY may be discussed in three forms: theoretical, practical, and as a process of transformation. The theoretical or speculative aspect survives today in theoretical physics. The practical aspect was the foundation of experimental physics. As a process of transformation, alchemy is still practiced in the Jungian school of depth psychology. The processes and symbolism of alchemy form a living link to the present. They spontaneously appear with their classic themes in the dreams and other deep subconscious expressions of modern people.

The redemption of the Divine by human consciousness was a theme basic to alchemy. Today this is widely expressed in pop psychology and New Age philosophy through seeing and connecting with the divinity within. The soul is conceived as a divine spark seeking experience in the creation before returning to its original home. The experience of God as imminent or within is a mystical point of view. As your soul comes closer to being one with that, you experience a greater sense of integration and wholeness. This return to the self or Higher Self is a very healing experience.

Alchemists employ the process of transmutation in an attempt to release and redeem a supreme value from its bondage in base matter, which is equivalent to the physical world. Perhaps what is most widely known of alchemists is that they sought to "turn lead into gold." In literal, physical terms this is still problematical. However, this process proves very possible on the psychological level. We may read the statement metaphorically where lead represents all of our neurotic attitudes and compulsive behaviors. Transmutation is similar to both the process and goal of therapy. Mostly this means paying attention to the many cues coming to the conscious from the unconscious through dreams, moods, behavior patterns, fantasies, etc. Gold represents self-realization.

Alchemical experiments begin with the base matter known as the *prima materia* (or first matter), which is the starting condition. In terms of therapy it is the presenting problem that the client would like to "fix." In this original condition you cannot distinguish between what belongs to the personality and what forces operating in your life are transpersonal—beyond personal control and responsibility.

In this psychologically immature state your ego cannot separate itself from the powers and abilities of the collective unconscious. This can lead to an egotistical orientation because the ego mistakes the dynamic forces of the subconscious for its own power. Through the process of psychological transformation, the ego learns its relative position as center of the conscious personality. However, it also learns that it is only a relatively minor part of that greater circle of the Self.

Carl Jung developed theories concerning the nature of the collective unconscious and its relationship to each individual's personal unconscious. The personal unconscious comes from your individual experiences and repressions, or painful experiences pressed back from awareness. On the other hand, the collective unconscious is an inherited legacy of all mankind that appears in the symbols of religion, the imagery of myth, and the nightly drama of our dreams.

Jung discovered a wealth of psychological truth in the images of alchemy. Consequently, depth psychology employs the language of alchemy to illuminate the natural transformation process in modern individuals. Alchemy is a process of self-transformation with the aim of creating a series of unions of various contending psychic substances. In other words, it heals internal conflicts.

These internal splits may be caused by the conflict of opposing conscious and subconscious dynamic forces. You as a personality may want and need certain things in your life, but an archetypal force acting through you with its own agenda may know nothing of these crucial human needs. It has its own aim. Here, the value of inner dialogue becomes important.

Some lives are disrupted by two conflicting subconscious forces. Mostly these can be characterized as conflicting subpersonalities like "the Judge and the Rebel," the "Critical Parent and Child," and so on. Here again, dialogue or listening and paying attention to these voices within has tremendous value.

The forces of consciousness are represented by the ego. The ego is the center of the personality complex, which includes your physical characteristics, emotions, intellect, and values. The Self is not only the metaphorical center of the subconscious, it is the center and circumference of the total individual. Its paradoxical nature is both personal and transpersonal. When we can experience transcendence of the mundane personality, we feel enriched and nourished and connected to the cosmos. This experience gives divine worth and meaning to our human nature, and dignity to our personal experience.

Both Jungian psychology and alchemy are methods of developing a certain type of relationship between the ego and the Self that helps to harmonize the whole being: the ego represents the tendency toward physical manifestation and attachment to the physical plane; the Self represents the tendency toward transcendence of physicality or movement into mystical states of consciousness.

In that condition known as *prima materia*, your ego cannot distinguish itself from the powerful patterns of the collective unconscious. To submit this material to the alchemical process means to apply conscious effort and attention to the task. In this process you find your own spirituality. You engage in a process of personal refinement where the goal is to free the Self or archetypal psyche from its contamination by the ego and its negative habit patterns. Paradoxically, since the ego is our conscious choice-maker, the ego must make a concerted effort to transcend itself. This process of ego-death can be frightening to someone with no conception of the beauties that lie beyond.

A person feeling stress from the problems of life may be forced into therapy by pressures beyond his control. But those in good psychological health can also benefit from an examination of their deepest selves. The problem is in knowing when, where, and how to begin! It cannot be done without some structuring of the cycle of unfolding transformation. You need a system of orientation in the inner world, just as in daily life. You can begin by making a positive commitment to approach the other side of your consciousness. If you muster positive energy, whether in the spirit of reverence or of discovery, you can experience unknown, hidden dimensions within.

The first plate of the Lambsprinck series shows that the initial stages of this process involve the recognition of the apparent opposites, Spirit and Soul. They find a common ground of expression and experience in your body, or matter in general.

The two fish swimming in opposite directions, represent the spirit/soul polarity. The water in which they swim may be alternately considered as the physical body, or the unconscious. The realm of psyche encompasses both. The goal of alchemy is the unification of Matter, Spirit, and Soul. In Western terms, this means healing the mind/body split brought about by the belief in original sin. This belief system sees the body as inherently evil rather than merely instinctual.

In the language of symbols, animal symbolism forms images which show the unconscious self manifesting through "animal impulses." A fish represents a very deep instinctual level, even more primitive than those symbolized by reptiles or mammals. This layer of the psyche consists largely of those feelings, beliefs, compulsions, and phobias that run counter to the so-called biological instincts. There are self-defeating or self-destructive urges that inhibit sexual pleasure, distort our appetites, or create life-threatening disease in us. Our sense of wholeness or integrity is disturbed by conflicting drives.

Two fish swimming in opposite directions in this ocean of body and psyche shows the paradoxical nature of symbols of wholeness. The fish represent the opposites to be united: soul and spirit. In this context soul is the urge to experience life in manifestation, and spirit the urge to transcend the chains of the physical. They also represent the male and female polarities of existence. Their union, induced by the alchemist through purposeful intent, is the goal of alchemy. This union occurs in the realm of the psyche which spans physical and spiritual reality. Through imagination the realities of inner life become just as "real" as the outside world.

The composition of the *ultima materia* (end result) and *prima materia* (beginning conditions) are essentially the same. In both states the ego and Self are fused. The major difference is that your ego in the final state has gained conscious awareness of its differences from the contents of the collective unconscious. The alchemist learns to distinguish himself from the various archetypes that lie in the depths of the psyche and influence daily life. The value of this pursuit is in uniting consciously with the wellsprings of Being. It is a healing, renewing experience.

The process of transformation, which begins in *prima materia* and culminates in the *ultima materia*, is known in alchemy as the Great Work. The corresponding process of psychological transformation is termed individuation, the process of moving toward Wholeness. They are analogous. The goal of this Great Work is to develop a firsthand, personal awareness of the transpersonal aspects of the psyche, or the hidden Self. The Self is only hidden because of the ego's unconscious identification with it. The ego may come to realize that everything in your psyche is not of its own making.

The entire spectrum of the relationship of your ego to the Self can be described in nine stages:

   1. Your ego is absent, totally identified with the unconscious, as in infancy.
   2. Just as you grow and develop physically, your ego rises and you learn to distinguish yourself from the environment.
   3. Your ego becomes aware of its emergent powers and explores love of self and parents.

4. Your ego stops focusing on making people respond and starts trying to make things.

5. The pangs of separation from the original condition of blissful wholeness are felt in the alienation of the adolescent identity crisis.

6. The ego begins yearning to recapture the sense of wholeness in love of the beloved and creativity.

7. Attachment to strictly personal needs is further dissolved by being a nurturing parent, teacher, sponsor, or mentor, and detachment from externals is experienced in mystic ecstasy.

8. The reign of the ego in consciousness ends in *illumination* for its destiny is to transcend itself.

9. The tyranny of the puny ego is over; it is again absent, having merged back into universal awareness, cosmic consciousness, unification (*ultima materia*).

This summary is synthesized from our study of human development in the works of Jung, Erickson, Piaget, and Gowan. It describes the emergence of consciousness from the original unconscious condition and the merging of personal consciousness in universal consciousness. It can form a blueprint for your own transformative process. The images of Lambsprinck amplify and shed light on this self-discovery formula. Other translations of this chapter speak of "cooking" the *prima materia*. The *prima materia* is all your uncooked raw emotion.

On this journey of inner discovery, the Self appears in many symbols or forms. These forms appear in a fairly predictable order in the beginning stages. The first stages always involve encounters with your social mask (*persona*), your dark side (*shadow*), and your inner femininity or masculinity (*anima/animus*). You might also meet such figures as the Wise Old Man, Trickster, Great Mother, Healer, and Inner Child. When these mysterious inner figures remain unconscious, we project their qualities onto those who provide a suitable "hook" for "my enemy," "my soulmate," "my wise teacher," and so on. In time, as a self-explorer you learn to distinguish these recurrent patterns from the personalities of the people you are involved with. You own your projections, that part of yourself you have given away so freely. The energy projected out comes back to you in an enriched inner life and your sense of wholeness is enhanced.

Another way these patterns lay claim to you and exert their influence is when your ego identifies with a specific archetype, one part of the Self. Then you perceive yourself as "the hero," or "the great lover," or "the teacher of wisdom." The ego gets all puffed up with the importance that really belongs to the archetype, and human values suffer .

The *prima materia* essentially represents the crossroads or crisis preceding a spiritual awakening. In this stage you are busy living ordinary life, taking it as it comes, attempting to fulfill personal desires, and carrying out social duties without much reflection. You may be religious but in a rather traditional, superficial way. But then something happens—disappointments, shocks, the death of someone close—that sets you seeking deeper meaning. Or the shift may be felt as a sense of "Is this all there is?" even if you have health and prosperity. Thus an ordinary person becomes a "seeker." You begin to question the meaning and purpose of your life, and suffering. Ordinary life seems empty and unreal, but you have not connected with what lies beyond. You may feel mentally unbalanced, uneasy, agitated. You seek escape through working harder, a hyperactive social life, or any new stimuli. Still the void cannot be filled—inward emptiness is painful and becoming intolerable. You are distracted but not relieved.

Preserving your old social image, with all its "shoulds" and "ought tos," like a robot, becomes impossible. As your conscience is awakened you may feel guilt, remorse, and shame. You judge yourself harshly and feel profound discouragement. Perhaps you even entertain ideas of suicide. Certainly there will be intellectual doubts and metaphysical problems. The emotional depression or the moral crisis may be emphasized at different times. The emotional issues are crying out to be dealt with through therapy, and moral crisis seeks resolution through finding your own relationship to divinity within.

Alchemy and individuation are essentially religious endeavors. One is a spiritual philosophy; the other a spiritual psychology. They are not ways of "fixing" yourself, by disposing of undesirable qualities and weaknesses. Rather, they are ways for you to come to conscious knowledge of the entire spectrum of your human possibilities. They are procedures for rebalancing psychic functioning and integrating the fragments of archetypal patterns that underlie human existence.

Individuation is not the road for all. Frequently those who choose to pursue it are forced toward it. They seek therapy because they have become dysfunctional due to depression, illness, stagnation, or breakdown of current adaptation to reality. The unconscious sends its message in a forceful way so the ego can no longer ignore it indefinitely. The ego's personal desires are supplanted by a process that seems irrational. Individuation arises out of the conflict between the ego and the unconscious, which always feels unknown or alien. You do not choose the path of individuation, but rather are chosen by it. If your ego can withstand the temptations, ordeals, and perils at the hands of the unknown, you are eventually rewarded with an expanded experience of self and rejuvenation, a rebirth. "Finding yourself" means self-acceptance based on what comes from within, not without.

The first encounter with the potencies of the collective unconscious comes with your *persona* or social mask. It is a defensive system that is largely influenced by your culture and represents your "image" or how you wish to be seen. "Putting up a front" may be a necessary adaptation to outer life. Just reflect on what you would like people to know about you and what you don't want them to know.

Your trouble comes if you identify exclusively with this facade and feel there is little to life other than "playing the role." Then you are no more than your job or avocations make you. You are a "human doing," not a "human being." This disastrous condition can cut you off from your unconscious roots and instinctual nature. Some people experience it as a mind/body split. The unconscious will attack from all sides in protest if you are caught in a narrow role of only mother, worker, student, or any other generic role lacking individuality. You feel like a cog in a machine.

The persona is a psychological complex that is very close to "normal" ego-consciousness. It is the outer personality you present to others. You can picture it imaginally as a mask of conformity that you use to adapt to everyday living. These masks can be learned early in life and are even used in families where we find, among others, the hero, caretaker, clown, black sheep, perfectionist, the placater, and the lost or invisible child in dysfunctional family systems. The defensive maneuvers we learn in childhood are carried over into adult life. They are not necessarily "true" to our core-being but are adaptations learned to survive trauma and/or crazy-making behavior by our adult caregivers.

Your ego chooses these adaptations to please others or protect you, and builds up a persona or false front to act as armor. The problem is, as impressionable children, we choose external cues from angry parents, dissatisfied teachers, demanding bosses, and jealous children. Over and over we get the message that we are crazy, stupid, bad, ugly, or unlovable. And, when some part of us believes those sick messages, we form a life with negative thinking and behavior patterns to conform to these expectations.

Such questions arise as: "Who am I?"; "What can I do to change?"; "What's wrong with me?"; "Why do I feel so bad?" These are precisely the symptoms of codependence, so frequently discussed in recovery literature. Codependence results when your primary caregivers are unable or unwilling to meet your childhood emotional needs. It feels like abandonment to your soul. Family therapists claim more than 95% of the population is plagued with these feelings of insecurity and inner turmoil.

Other symptoms that occur include control issues; ignoring your own interests and needs; fear of rejection and anger; taking too much responsibility for others; obsessive thinking; difficulty making choices; being out of touch with your feelings; addiction to chemicals, sensations, sex, or relationships; denying reality with fantasies; problems with intimacy; and chronic physical ailments.

Society can also teach sick behavior. Some individuals respond to the demands of society for "normal" behavior by learning to suppress their inwardly held values and feelings and doubting their own perceptions. Most people's need for social acceptance outweighs their need for individuality . . . at least for a time. We want to be appropriate to our social class and these obsessions for conformity are reflected in fashion, religion, education, and entertainment. We seek common experiences. We have a strong desire to "fit in" and fear rejection, isolation, or abandonment.

Your persona shows in your special costumes or uniforms and in your chosen lifestyle. Your group participations effect your attitudes, perception, motivation, and emotions. You may come to adopt attitudes dominant among members of groups you move in. You may be set apart in a social class by economics, politics, beliefs, or prestige. Membership in a particular social class partly determines your individual behavior and your personal feelings of power may be affected. Stratification by wealth, honor, and power are social phenomena. Implicit are the ideas of "will" and "influence."

Social mobility may be both upward or downward. This yields a fragmented system of subcultures. We are so conformist, even our eccentrics form their own subcultures. The American Dream includes the work ethic, political and economic freedoms, property ownership, local autonomy, and equality of opportunity. Many find that the modern social structure no longer provides a means for attaining all these values and begin to despair. The work-a-day world seems empty and meaningless.

Three classic personas emerge in this environment:

   1) The person as packaged commodity, ready to be "sold" to others as a "dressed-for-success" conformist. Acceptance is based on superficial conformity rather than on genuinely personal qualities.
   2) The placater emulates rather than initiates, looking to others

rather than internalized values as cues for appropriate behavior.

3) The corporate clone is so geared to organizational life that bureaucratic precepts guide his entire personal and family life.

The phenomena of the "yuppie" lifestyle epitomizes the modern quest to sustain a lifestyle that is not innovative or distinctive, but suppresses individuality, freedom, and creativity. When this status seeking becomes oppressive or hollow we seek a transformation of our personal identity. We begin to consider "following our bliss" as Joseph Campbell put it. You can increase your awareness of persona by contemplating the question "Who am I?" Record your several answers. You may find conflicting self-concepts. Another exercise is to describe yourself in a self-portrait, or as others may see you. You may find conflicting self-concepts.

For more direct inner experience, make some quiet time to initiate an internal dialogue with your *persona*. Dim the lights, and use deep breathing to relax yourself, but have materials handy to record your experience. Let your rational consciousness relax and move to the imaginal level where *"persona"* is a living reality. *Persona* lies at the threshold of the subconscious, combining inner and outer.

"A cruel black dragon lurks in the wood"

PLATE 2

On this day the Wise agree
That a wild beast walks in the forest;
It is quite black all over.
When its head is cut off
The blackness will disappear completely
Changing to snow white.

Understood correctly,
The blackness is called the head of the Raven;
But as soon as the blackness disappears
And the whiteness shows
It is called "robbed of its head."

I believe the Wise
Are heartily glad
When the black smoke finally dissipates.

Yet they keep this secret closely guarded
That no foolish man may know it,
Only allowing it to be written about
for the benefit of their Sons.

What is given of God
Becomes reserved.

Therefore one should say nothing about it
While God would have it concealed.

My son, be it quickly understood,
A cruel black dragon lurks in the wood.

Putrefaction.

Chapter 2: Shadow

The Nigredo

THE *nigredo* or blackening phase of the alchemical process implies a gloomy time of depression. This time of life feels inauspicious. You may feel unlucky, caught in a black mood whose origin may seem difficult to pinpoint. This is because your current ego attitudes are outdated, and, lacking adaptability, you feel stuck. These feelings may come about from an overload of stress in daily life. As these feelings become more intolerable the notion that life is meaningless comes to the fore. It is simply that life as your ego has known it in the past is outmoded. The subconscious begins to revolt, seeking a psychological revolution in attitudes. If you listen to the voice within your depression, you come to realize that you must willingly subject yourself to change.

This decision to subject yourself to change may be considered a spiritual awakening. You realize that your essential being is the material to be transformed via the alchemical process. To proceed further, you need to understand that the black substance is your own shadow archetype, or the repressed contents of your personal unconscious. Until you are willing to look at your unlived potential both for evil and for good, you may be stuck in a state of melancholy, sleeplessness, or senseless hyperactivity. You realize that "something is wrong," but can't quite identify what it might be.

Many individuals experience a period of depression or melancholia between the ages of twenty-eight to thirty and again from fifty-five to sixty. Astrologically, this age group experiences "the Saturn return," the twenty-eight year cyclical return of the planet to its original position in the natal chart. Classically, it is a time of disappointment, divorce, soul-searching, reassessment of values, and reorientation in life. The planet Saturn puts the accent on responsibility, in this case your responsibility to yourself to fulfill your potential. Finally, you are truly grown up, and your destiny begins to take *form*. You may be pressured into it even if you resist, and this is that black mood's positive intent.

Jung recommended no one embark on the path of individuation before the age of thirty. Why? Because until that time it is best for the ego to invest emotional energy in building security, family, and career in order to create a solid foundation for spirituality. Then one may be sure it is no premature,

35

escapist transcendentalism. At first the *nigredo* (black state) may be experienced as restriction, but it can also feel liberating. At least now you begin to know what you should be doing and this can help you feel freer within. You may even get a glimpse of the light, of superconscious levels, which precipitates the crisis of spiritual awakening. This produces a spontaneous experience of unity, which passes quickly.

This stage of discomfort with the status quo is quite necessary to initiate the alchemical process, for you must find the intrinsic value and meaning within your depressive cycle. True, you will have to withstand a chaotic state of conflict among hostile psychic forces. You will feel a strong backward pull toward the unconsciousness of the motivating factors of your behavior. Your emotions may feel deadened, and you are dissociated or on the verge of a nervous breakdown. Life as you have known it is falling apart. You are grieving, mourning the death of your old self, and may not yet even know it.

In this plate the dragon is a mythological being which symbolizes processes devoid of emotional response. There is always psychic suffering when you "fall down," partly from self-judgement. "Being down in the dumps" may become a lifestyle if you find no structured method of moving past this point in your personal growth. You may remain a depressive, possibly volcanic personality, because so much rage, aggression, and self-hatred has been bottled up inside. However, by just simply "picking yourself back up," you instinctively activate inner healing resources. But to do this you must stay in touch with your therapeutic process.

There is a passage in the alchemical text *Aurelia Occulta Philosophorum*, where the transformative substance of the *nigredo* state describes itself:

> I am an infirm and weak old man, surnamed the dragon; therefore am I shut up in a cave, that I may become ransomed by the kingly crown. . . . A fiery sword inflicts great torments on me; death makes weak my flesh and bones. . . . My soul and my spirit depart; a terrible poison, I am likened to the black raven, for that is the wages of sin; in dust and earth I lie, that out of Three may come One. O soul and spirit leave me not, that I may see again the light of day, and the hero of peace whom the whole world shall behold may arise from me.

"The head of the Raven" is another traditional name for the *nigredo*. It corresponds to the encounter with the shadow. The ego and the shadow must eventually be reconciled. Your restlessness and disorientation come from your experience of conflict between conscious and unconscious drives. The unconscious must be transformed. The Self, symbolized as a dragon, devours itself and dies, only to rise again when the work is perfected.

This illustration shows your ego as a martial figure with his sword (rational intellect) in direct confrontation with the shadow-aspect of the unconscious. This plate represents the beginning of the descent into darkness on the path of individuation. That darkness is simply the unknown of your own deep subconscious mind. In your own depths you confront that which you have previously rejected and suppressed, both evil and good.

As long as your soul struggles in the *nigredo*, you take things too literally. You may think you are approaching your problem pragmatically, assessing the facts, and coming up with concrete solutions. Really, you may be stuck in spiritual materialism, rather than reading your symptoms metaphorically. You may seek a quick fix, such as an antidepressant pill. However, you would serve yourself better by extracting the symbolic aspects of your condition and giving yourself a new perspective on the meaning of life. In this way you address your core issues rather than merely your symptoms of discomfort.

Typical manifestations of this stage include long dreams and nightmares (when you can actually sleep), confusions, and a drained or depressed mental attitude that creates inertia. You honor the Self and your own wholeness when you look at the *nigredo* symbolically as a meaningful part of the mysterious process of inner transformation. However, you miss this point and stay stuck in the *nigredo* when you look for what is wrong with you outside of yourself. Something is "wrong" inside, and without this realization nothing will alter your depression. You may blame your psychosomatic aches and pains on organic or neurological problems. You may seek relief through drugs, body work, aerobics, or dance therapy. But if you fail to recognize that you suffer from sickness of the soul, neither vitamins, drugs, nor exercise will cure what ails you.

In the *nigredo* state, your *élan vital* or life energy has been pulled into the unconscious leaving your ego frustrated, discontented, and isolated. You may feel this emptiness and sterility precisely because you have placed too much emphasis on achievement in the outer world and gotten out of balance. This leaves your soul cut off from the well-springs of life. Your feeling of being drained or overextended may become so powerful that you experience a breakdown that imposes a period of time for introversion and recovery of energy reserves.

When you see through the literal aspects of depression to the value of this feeling you can experience the meaningfulness of the feelings of meaning-lessness. The paradoxical value of this is that attaching meaning to depression allows an emotional participation that unblocks the flow of psychic energy. You can regain your sense of meaning in life, and this realization is the starting point for inner discovery. Examples of this process from literature include Dante's *Inferno*, Melville's *Moby Dick*, and Fowles' *The Magus*.

If you can see that the world is beautiful, but have lost the ability to feel that beauty, of course your moods are going to swing from sullen inertia to active despair. If there is seemingly no meaning in life, why exist at all! You feel fragmented, alienated from yourself. This is a major reason many seek therapy or a mystical path of renewal.

When you understand the dynamics of the *nigredo*, the depression begins to abate. But in order for this to happen, you must accept the blackness as your own instead of blaming it on outside situations or other people. Then you begin to discover that it is your own withdrawal and loss of feeling about your own shadow nature that is the source of the darkness. When you turn your attention toward it, you see you are not suffering a merely personal ill, but one with transpersonal dimensions. In other words, this is a plight common to all of mankind and a milestone on the path of individuation. It is a natural part of development.

When your ego can no longer pursue only its selfish concerns and addictive demands, the Self forces you into a depression to shake up the stagnant order of things. It brings a burning awareness of your shortcomings and inadequacies. To get to the root of these, you need to process old traumas and negative core beliefs that severely limit you. The Self appears on your inner stage as the shadow and confronts you with your inferior traits.

These shadow traits include all those that tend to keep you from realizing your unique potential for personal fulfillment. Cowardice, laziness, ambivalence, rashness, dishonesty, envy, greed, lust, vanity, and attachment, and other self-indulgent tendencies will have to be faced directly. The narcissistic shadow is the diametrical opposite of our positive assets. If you are compulsively organized in daily life, the shadow tends to let things slide, for example. If you are puritanical, the shadow is promiscuous.

The shadow is not necessarily acted out in self-destructive behavior, but if it has no means of expression your ego cannot transform beyond this phase of development. Some form of inner dialogue is useful. You must come to a conscious understanding of those things you have repressed and have not been able or dared to live out. As an aspect of the Self, the shadow embodies the primitive, dark background from which we all emerge. But only the ego passes negative judgement on the shadow. The Self embraces all opposites, including good and bad.

In highly religious persons, who tend to overidentify with the great good of the Light, the shadow may assume the form of a devilish adversary and produce hypocrisy. It attacks with compulsions from below producing behaviors such as those seen in Jim Jones, Jimmy Swaggart, and Jim Baker. What may start as good intentions become perverted. But in the broader reality, the shadow gives human existence body and depth, if consciously integrated. In physics, the brighter the light, the deeper the shadows which are cast. The shadow embodies our ulterior motives and pathologies.

If you do not take responsibility for consciously becoming aware of your shadow traits, you will find them projected onto others of the same sex in your environment. You may feel an irrational, instinctive hatred for virtual strangers. On the collective level this manifests as racial prejudice. When you feel any emotion that seems highly exaggerated, it usually means you are projecting. When that extreme emotion is irrational vehemence, you are projecting your own repressed weakness onto others. To do this you must deny a part of yourself and you cannot experience wholeness. Therefore, in order to continue your process of transformation, you must come to an awareness of your particular shadow characteristics. If you reach down deeply enough, you will find that the shadow is not only negative, but also holds your unlived potential for positive change. As you re-own this lost part of yourself, you open a channel between the conscious and the superconscious levels, between the ego and the Self. This experience can bring a flood of light, joy, and energy, which brings temporary release from the depression. Even your psychosomatic symptoms may vanish suddenly.

If your personality is not well grounded you may not be able to assimilate an inflow of light and strength. The alchemist must balance intellect and emotion by using imagination in a controlled way to digest this sudden illuminating insight. When your ego reacts with egotism or conceit it confuses itself with the power of the Self. This confusion of levels has the unfortunate effect of creating a self-glorification that is much like mistaking a soul for God. Of course, it is divine, but limited in comparison. Should you become bedazzled by divine truths beyond your mental power to digest, you may become self-deluded and/or victimized by a cult. You need to develop your powers of discrimination. Megalomania is extreme egotism that can lead a person to act out the role of prophet or savior, spurred on by the excitement of his or her own inner awakening.

At this stage you may begin experiencing paranormal phenomena: ESP, clairvoyance, or synchronicities (meaningful coincidences). You may have visions of divine beings, hear voices, or dabble with automatic writing. Be sure to examine any messages of uncommon origin with discrimination. Any messages exalting your personality should be automatically suspect.

Other reactions to spiritual awakening may occur later as doubts fall away and new inner security is found. You may be elated for a time, but your personal self was only temporarily overpowered and not permanently transformed. When the spiritual force seems to ebb away, you may be in for trouble as your ego seeks to reassert its dominion. The trap is to judge yourself even more harshly for being merely human. You have not fallen lower than when you began, but you may feel the full fury of the lower drives. When their uncontrolled expression is threatened, they may rear their ugly heads with more force than ever.

Another reaction is to deny the value and reality of your spiritual awakening. The inner critic or skeptic creates doubts and attempts to label it as fantasy. With bitterness and sarcasm you may rebuke your aspirations and ideals. But when you have had a transformative vision, you cannot deny it for long and remain healthy. It brings more depression, a sense of unworthiness, and the feeling that you are damned. *Nigredo* can be likened to "the descent into hell."

All those in the arts and sciences experience periods of aridity and inability to work. When no new inspirations come, you may feel cut off from the source of creative flow. The depression and restlessness that result may lead to alcohol or drugs, until or unless the sudden flow of inspiration brings a sense of renewal.

You need to be aware of the true nature of this crisis and realize that an exalted state cannot be maintained forever. It is no fall from grace, but a natural happening that gives you emotional and mental relief from the tensions of inspiration and illumination. After all, you can only digest so much change at once. Instead of staying stuck in the depression you can continue on the path to self-realization.

"A Stag and Unicorn in the forest go"

PLATE 3

The Wise truly say
That two wild beasts lurk in the forest:
One is beautiful, well-formed and spirited,
A great strong antlered stag;
The other is a radiant white unicorn.

Both lie hidden in the forest;
We call the man insightful
Who can spy and catch them.

Here and everywhere the Masters concisely reveal
That two beasts move through the forest;
Yet the forest must be understood to be one thing.

First, to reach the root of all things,
Matter will be called the forest,
So shall we know and understand things rightly.

The Unicorn stands for Spirit;
The Stag answers to no other name
Than Soul and none can deny it.

Now it is true that he, who by Art,
Knows how to tame them,
Leading them out of the forest,
Yet driving them close together,
Would be called a Master.

Such a man has found the Golden Fleece.
So now he may triumph,
And might govern over great Augustus.

Now it is important that you know
A Stag and Unicorn in the forest go.

Soul and Spirit exist in Matter.

Chapter 3: Anima

The Union of Opposites

ABOUT ten of the fifteen Lambsprinck illustrations overtly depict the dualistic nature of the Self. The Self embodies the union of opposites on both the personal and cosmic scale. It presents itself through such classic symbols of paradox as life/death, time/eternity, good/evil, and masculine/feminine. In this plate, the contents of the unconscious are shown as vegetative and warm-blooded life. The stag, a real creature, is feminine and represents the soul. The unicorn, a mythical or imaginal being, stands for spirit. It is the masculine penetrating force. The forest is the body.

The unicorn represents "one-pointedness." Conscious intent and subconscious only collide when your rational mind wants to clamp down on unreason. The crisis, symbolized in the previous picture as confrontation, will abate if the rationality of the ego does not continue to interfere too much. Primarily *because* they are in conflict, the opposites will draw together over a period of time. What appeared to foretell death and destruction now indicates a possibility of harmonious blending.

In physics this process is called covalent bonding, where elements unite because of mutual deficiencies. The whole is greater than the sum of its parts because of a synergistic quality. This quality of "wholeness" is represented in psychology as the archetype of the Self. Your internal conflicts may be creative as well as destructive. Limited conflict, seen in terms of the whole, may be necessary for future development. Your conscious ego may not even acknowledge the autonomy of the unconscious, and it certainly cannot determine the source or goal of on-going psychic processes. Furthermore, if you over-analyze this process in yourself, you might inhibit the transformation.

At this stage, you need to develop an ego that can not only penetrate, but also diffuse its awareness. This flexible ego can form a more harmonious relationship with subconscious processes. It does not abort the transformation in the middle of the process through wrong value judgements and interference. The totality of the psyche has its own aims, which are not necessarily those of the individual ego. Psychic activity is paradoxical in nature. It looks both forward and backward. Its manifestations are both "good" and "bad." Thus it represents itself in terms of polarities. When the opposites unite in your psyche's depths, neither side is given preeminence.

45

The path through the opposites may be termed "the Middle Way" and is seen in examples from many cultures. For example, it is represented in the Chinese concept of the Tao with its components yin and yang. The dictum of Greek philosophy to "know thyself" springs from Apollonian religion, which asserts that "the Mean is best." This is the basis of the Golden Mean in art and philosophy. In the mystical symbol of the Kabbalistic Tree, the mean is symbolized by the Middle Pillar. More recently the opposites were united in the philosophical formula of Hegel: thesis-antithesis and synthesis. The path through the opposites is also symbolized as "walking the razor's edge."

Depth psychology has the aim of religion, coupled with the method of science. You can develop a love for psychological truth coupled with a scientific spirit of inquiry by delving into your own depths in this special way. This brings you the possibility of increased understanding and expanded awareness, a synthesis of the values of soul and spirit. Self-knowledge gives you some degree of freedom from selfish ego-centered desires and helps you develop philosophical detachment from the ups and downs of life.

When your ego surrenders to the transpersonal concerns of the total Self, you learn to accept your lot in life. This allows the creative spirit within to begin its transformative work. This process is reflected in your body through the harmonization of the sympathetic and parasympathetic nervous systems. When you function at an optimal level there is a balance between the tensions produced in living and your ability to relax and rejuvenate yourself.

In order to transform past the *nigredo* phase of melancholy you may take up a conscious dialogue with your shadow, and become aware of your unconscious projections and identifications. This running commentary with your shadow is the only way to fix its character in your conscious mind and gain insight into your depths. True, this self-examination may be painful, but to know yourself you must become aware of the contradictions between the parts of you that feel "I want" and "I ought."

The path of equilibrium between the opposites requires you to keep an attitude of open-mindedness and wholeness. There are four characteristic responses to this internal conflict of opposites which may be summarized as follows:

   1) Mood swings, attitude reversals, or conversion experiences show
   that you are polarized and fluctuating widely from one extreme to
   another. The swings may be of longer or shorter duration. When the

pendulum swings, you are identified with one facet of a complementary pair. You need to find the middle ground. In psychology this oscillation phenomena is called *enantiodromia*.

2) If you feel *ambivalence*, you are holding conflicting feelings simultaneously. Again, this is no median position. You remain in discomfort, brought to a standstill. In this stagnant condition, you feel incapable of action. You are stuck.

3) *Denial* is another means of reacting to the opposites. It is an escapist attitude which might provide a means of coping, but not of transformation. You may regress back into identification with your social mask. Try as you might to "keep it together" and "save face," you can't repress the conflict indefinitely.

4) *True compromise* is the result of a genuine resolution of the opposites. In terms of settling internal conflicts, this means both your ego and other subpersonalities make concessions in favor of the whole Self. The price of transformation is a regeneration of the personality. You must actively remove obstacles to the inflow of superconscious energies to experience self-realization. As your higher functions develop, the ego learns to let the Higher Self work, and must endure the pressure and pain of the transformative process.

Experiencing the union of opposites, you alternate between light and darkness, joy and suffering. Your attention is so engrossed with your inner process that you may find yourself impaired in your daily activities. Casual observers may think you are deteriorating and judge you harshly. They may find your spiritual ideals too impractical. This criticism hurts, but it also tends to arouse your doubts and discourages you. This test allows you to practice inner independence, and inner strength. However, you cannot remain in a cocoon during your period of transition. In fact, when Jung went through this stage, he found that the only thing that kept him grounded was his family, professional life, and social duties. You may feel like you are leading a double life, but you must go on through your depression, exhaustion, and ennui. Another common mistake at this phase is to inhibit or forcefully repress the sexual and aggressive urges. This just intensifies the conflict, and usually comes from religious attitudes about what is "bad" or "sinful." The unconscious still feels the conflict and produces feelings of ambivalence, or you swing from suppression to uncontrolled expression of your drives. This may be cathartic, but creates new conflicts between drives, and in your social adjustment and personal relations. However, these oscillations may have the positive psychological value of providing you with conscious realizations about your shadow nature. You learn to see how the shadow compensates for and deflates your egotistical self-image. In fact, it is the nature of psychological complexes to suddenly switch into their opposites. This is the basis of rehabilitation. Reform implies the reforming of attitudes and thought patterns, influencing your values and priorities. The law of compensation is the basis of "rebirth" phenomena and represents a return swing of the pendulum. The Middle Way encourages a balanced personality rather than radical mood swings.

The true compromise lies in the harmonious integration of all your drives into your total personality. In therapy, you can personify these drives as subpersonalities and bring them to a round table or conference room so they can coordinate their efforts and find their own levels. This will free up a lot of your energy that formerly went into conflict. The judge and rebel within are readily seen. Sometime, when your inner judge is holding court, unmask that judge and see who lies behind this punitive force in you. Usually it is the internal parent who administers the rules and laws. The wimp is the opposite side of the rebel. Your rebel establishes and maintains your individuality, but the wimp will comply to win love, acceptance, and approval. You may also consult your perfectionist, saboteur, warrior, wizard, and others.

Each of the subpersonalities responsible for your problem behavior has a counterpart in the superconscious. You can learn how to connect these opposites together to transmute the lower drive into the higher. This process is called sublimation. According to Jung, for example, the ideal of spiritual striving for the heights is always linked with the materialistic, earthbound passion for control. The archetype of the Self expresses this paradox through radically opposite changes in your conscious attitude. These 180-degree changes of attitude are to be expected as normal. Contradictory attitudes will intrude suddenly from the unconscious in the midst of daily life. There is a way out of this philosophical dilemma if you remain true to the Self. Even if your former ego trips become the source of your shame, you can use them for impetus to change. You cannot "tame the opposites," but you can allow them to equilibrate one another. They need to interrelate as if they are distinct but conjoined, like at the round table discussion. Another exercise might simply be to meditate on balancing each thought against its opposite.

If you pay attention, the Self will guide you to the true compromise by presenting transforming images in your imagination and dreams. By providing yourself time for waking dreams you can foster the process within you. It is precisely these symbols that unite the opposites for you.

The symbols come spontaneously from your subconscious but are perceived consciously as meaningful or valuable. It is not rationally understood, but unfolds over time. Your integration is facilitated by the activation of the superconscious functions as you realize the Self. Your larger and higher interests act like a magnet to raise the psychic energy invested in your lower drives to the spiritual level. The ego cooperates when it contributes its will to the process of harmonious integration.

Symbols hint at a mystery but never directly reveal it. They hold great depth of meaning, which is only limited by your ability to interpret it. Symbols mediate, or form a bridge, between your logical, rational mind and the subjective, intuitive mind. The symbol stands for what you cannot yet conceptualize. It has a subtle reality but seems "alive" as you experience it firsthand. Symbols undergo transformation, switching from one form to another, sometimes very rapidly in the therapeutic process. Thus, the rhythm of your inner changes is revealed to your conscious mind. You have a window on the tensions and release of your own subconscious processes, but only if you will to pay attention. As Lambsprinck said, "You must will to seize the noble fruit."

This symbol-forming function of the psyche has been called the transcendent function, Higher Self, or Holy Guardian Angel. It functions as an inner guide. It has the ability to synthesize and harmonize pairs of opposites in a symbol your rational ego could never invent. It creates a mode of transition from one set of attitudes to the next.

Putting your attention on the transforming symbols helps you overcome compulsive behavior arising in your complexes. You may choose to use it to mobilize both your conscious and unconscious energies to change yourself. You take responsibility for your internal changes rather than projecting them onto the environment and trying to rationalize your negative behavior. The more you value your symbols, the better they work for you. The alchemist was devoted to the discovery of the meaning of precisely these kinds of symbols. The alchemist not only gives himself over to the process, but preserves his psychic life by containing it in the Hermetic vessel. In other words, he pays attention to and meditates on the symbols presented in dreams, attitudes, and behavior. So, you might consider keeping a dream journal, recording your nightly sojourns.

At this stage of the transformation process, the opposites of the deep Self appear as your inner mate. A man's inner feminine self is termed *anima*, the Latin word for soul; a woman's masculine component is called *animus*, the Latin word for spirit. The inner mate is extremely important for further growth. By connecting with it you gain a valuable soul-guide to your inner depths. They reflect your image of an idealized member of the opposite sex, and may be projected outward onto someone you love instantly and deeply. If this happens, at some point you need to re-own this projection and come to know that inner mate as a separate relationship.

These soul-figures embody your latent capacity for expression and realization of the traits you normally consider reserved for members of the opposite sex. Thus, a man's *anima* might represent the capacity for being sensitive to other's feelings or his receptive nature. On the other hand, the *animus* might lead a woman into the outer world and promote her ability for focused, rational thinking. On this level of experience there is a blending of archetypal realities and individual experience. You can achieve a form of sacred marriage with your inner mate, known in alchemy as the *coniunctio*, a union which produces a *Magical Child* that symbolizes your potential for realization of the Higher Self.

As a soul-guide, a man's *anima* may dampen down his compulsiveness with her inherent tendency toward inhibition. Through this balancing, impulsive behavior is transmuted into spiritual potential when you attend to the elusive intuitions coming from her within. This is an example of the same forces depicted by the stag and the unicorn. They temper one another. When you personify your soul-guide in human form, the stag transforms into the symbol of the Virgin.

This "virgin taming the unicorn" is another famous alchemical theme concerning the active and passive nature of the Self. This feminine aspect of the Self brings the wild and free, but undisciplined, urges into relation with the reality needs of your ego. At the same time it helps you submit to the transpersonal totality of the psyche.

Man's unicorn nature is tamed when his wild, self-indulgent willfulness and arrogance are balanced by the gentle admonitions of his feminine guiding principle. The illusory defense, self-sufficiency, over-rational tendency, and rationalizations of the shadow behavior, are no longer acceptable as your self-image. At this point you can muster your energy for change.

In Jungian psychology, a "virgin" is not a woman who hasn't known sexual activity. Rather, she is a woman who is complete in herself, a symbol of feminine wholeness. She belongs to herself and functions as an independent entity uncontaminated by masculine attitudes. An actual woman may serve this function of soul-guide for a man, but only if she has a high degree of psychological awareness and is balanced herself.

Jung summarizes this stage by stating that "since the soul animates the body, just as the soul is animated by spirit, she tends to favour the body and everything bodily, sensuous, and emotional." Jung advises us to re-own that projection: "In modern terms it would be a turning away from the sensuous reality, a withdrawal of the fantasy-projections." In other words, it means introversion, introspection, meditation, and the careful investigation of desires and their motives. The reuniting of the spiritual position with the body obviously means that the insights gained should be made real. An insight might just as well remain in abeyance if it is simply not used.

From this point on there will be times when the flow of superconscious energies is easy and abundant. You must allow it to flow through in a balanced manner, circulating it through every aspect of your being. Otherwise you will feel too scattered from nervous excitement; or if you bottle it up, you may put too much pressure on your overloaded nervous system. Use this energy for your regeneration in creativity and service.

For many individuals these transformations happen in a gradual, harmonious way, without producing any severe symptoms. Still, adjustment periods are required. Any adverse reactions like nervousness or emotional upset are temporary. In fact, you may experience many regressions in the service of self-realization. They seem like steps backward, but are not. The renewed inflow of superconscious energies means powerful visionary experiences and inspiration. Use your vision, or dream frequently, keeping it before your inner eye. Connect with your inner joy, serenity, security, empowerment, discrimination, and love.

"A male and female stand hidden in darkness"

PLATE 4

The Wise give us to understand
That two strong lions wander the valley.
Male and female stand hidden in darkness
And must be discovered by Art.

These creatures are terrible and savage,
Of infinite energy, and untamed;
Snare them with wisdom and cunning.

He who knows how to tame and hold them,
Driving them back into the forest,
One can truly say of him
That he holds the Crown in another place,
Gained with glory to this day.

A great miracle may seem performed,
That from two lions are joined into one.

Spirit and Soul must be joined together,
And connected with their Matter.

"A male and female stand hidden in darkness."

Chapter 4: Animus

Participation Mystique

T HE lines from the text, "Male and female stand hidden in darkness and must be discovered by Art," show that this illustration continues the theme of the union of opposites. Each of us contains our inner partner of the opposite sex in our subconscious, and it is our psychological imperative to become aware of this inner guiding principle. This is a difficult task which requires commitment and may truly be considered an "Art."

In both plates 3 and 4, the *anima* and *animus* are symbolized by animals because they represent such a purely instinctual level of existence. If conscious awareness of *anima* and *animus* reached a more refined level, the image would be a human figure. However, plate 4 does show some progress in the situation, since now the masculine and feminine polarities are represented as members of the same species. The deep Self reveals its paradoxical nature as a lion and lioness.

In alchemy, the lion, or "royal" beast, is a frequent synonym for the archetype of the unconscious. Here, the lion is a transmutation of the devouring, predatory monster who first appeared as the dragon. Since the lion is "King of Beasts," it may be taken as representing all of the subhuman forces. "Taming the lion" means assimilating all the wild dangerous forces in nature to the uses of the creative imagination. This furthers the process of individuation. Man has dominion or subconscious direction over all subhuman life forms. This includes physical animals as well as our own "animalistic" instinctual patterns of behavior.

The fiery lions are meant to express the passionate emotions that both men and women experience prior to the recognition of unconscious psychological forces. Where there is insufficient adaptation to a situation, there is likelihood of emotional outbursts. If your ego is unaware of the needs of the unconscious, it carries a burden of guilt and responsibility for forces beyond its control. For example, if you project your inner needs and drives onto your beloved, you subconsciously expect the beloved to fulfill you. If (or *when*) this does not occur, you may become resentful, frustrated, demanding, or manipulative.

These uncontrollable displays of emotion are essentially bestial. People in this state are best approached with the attitude of an animal trainer. The alchemist seeks to "capture" and subdue these rampant impulses to further self-understanding. By taking back the responsibility for your own *anima/ animus* nature, you free your loved ones from an impossible burden. You can choose to submit your bad temper to the tempering heat of the alchemical process.

By developing an identification with your objective Observer Self, you can detach yourself from the wild oscillations of your shifting moods. In this manner, the observer unites yet transcends the opposites, and reminds you that you are more than your body, emotions, thoughts, and behaviors. Through the process of disidentifying from your subpersonalities, you learn to realign with your true Self. The split within you is replaced by a sense of integration, or enhancement. Only split-off parts of yourself are emotionally over-reactive. Partial selves are there to remind you that you are hung-up on certain negative patterns. The positive intent of the pattern can be met in other, creative ways. Then the subpersonality will fade into the background. Your negative behavior is transformed.

The Observer Self gives you a wider perspective on your situation, so you find more clarity. This impersonal self balances the attitudes of the personal self. It is your superconscious ability for philosophical detachment and allows insight into the illusory nature, or *maya*, of life in your physical form with limited awareness and perceptions. If you can adopt a wholistic perspective you move beyond dualistic consciousness automatically. As Observer you are *in* the situation but can also rise above it. Identified only with your ego, you remain trapped in the lower self. Try stepping outside of your emotional reactions and seeing them from a wider point of view. How do they relate to your growth process? As you observe, you operate from your higher, spiritual Self, which is androgynous.

Around midlife, both genders begin showing characteristics of the opposite sex. Women typically become more independent and strong-minded, and men more emotionally responsive, connective, and sensitive to others around them. Some people experience excitement in pursuing their missing personality parts, yet others just freeze up. These new potentials can seem frightening, alien, and dangerous. Your masculinity or femininity may seem threatened.

The higher your sense of self-esteem and well-being, the better positioned you are to welcome both dimensions into your life. As a woman, you can be loving and empathetic, but also knowledgeable, courageous, and ambitious. If you are a man you may suddenly find that you are more comfortable with intimacy, and intent on pursuing that. However, some make the error that these qualities are to be found outside themselves, in a new partner.

The true goal is to incorporate effectively the primary characteristics of your sexual opposite. Women can learn to admit and fulfill their ambitions, and men can learn to become more comfortable with intimacy. Though taught to shut off feelings from an early age, you can make the turn around and overcome your cultural stereotypes. By breaking through your confinements, you truly become more of a man or woman, a more whole human being. Our emerging cultural ideals and role models are the nurturing man and the courageous woman.

You need to examine the basis of your own drives and passions concerning the opposite sex. You can't even begin this process without being in a real relationship that provides feedback for your consideration. Many times our worst problem behaviors lie in our own psychological blind spot. The incidents of daily life provide you with ample opportunity to reflect on your unrealistic and conformist attitudes and behavior toward your beloved.

Anima/animus bears strongly on two important issues in your life: your sexuality and your creativity. Both are concerned intimately with the union of opposites into something that harmonizes both. Both sexuality and creativity result mainly from the combination of your conscious will with subconscious instinctual drives. Their harmonious combination yields fulfilling physical and aesthetic experiences. There is a relationship between conscious use of creative imagination and the subconscious generation of mental imagery useful in creative living or problem-solving.

In this illustration, the forest again symbolizes the world "out there" or the body. When you are involved in the transformative process, you do not become indifferent to the world of material things. You do not forsake your interest in external life for the fascinating realm of internal reality. You strike a balance between the two that is enriching. Things in your environment probably won't change much, but your attitude toward them certainly does. Your projections hide reality from you. You automatically attribute your unknown inner reality to people and things in your environment. This subjective filtering influences your choices and life-changing decisions. The opposite of unconscious compulsion is creative choice-making. You can play many roles in life with integrity if you identify with your core self for grounding balance. This includes both positive and negative traits, but without swinging to extremes.

Your ego cannot simply, however, decide to quit projecting, since the process is natural and spontaneous. Try as you might, you could never remove all your projections from the outer world. But you can gain awareness of the main archetypal forces that are most easily understood, and it is these that most often wreak havoc in your personal life. Many archetypes operate through you, and you must decide whether you will consciously relate to them or not. Your personality may have far different needs and goals than these eternal forces, and usually they do not know what you need either for security or survival. They will even threaten the life of the body to fulfill their aims, for they never feel the hand of death. By taking back your subjective projections, derived from age-old patterns within, you help decrease the emotional pollution in your environment.

As you learn to recognize and assimilate your projections, your relationship to the world is changed. Your identification with objects, your roles, other people, and your possessions may border on what is known as *participation mystique*. It is a way of being involved with externals to the point where they seem to exert a magical effect over you. If you use people or objects to mood-alter yourself, they possess you, and you can't possibly relate to them rationally. You have literally invested your energy in something other than yourself . . . and have given a piece of yourself away.

Mutual projections by lovers can result in all sorts of folly and shared delusions. Frequently people fall in love with those who have traits they would like to actualize in themselves. Instead of manifesting that, we let the other carry those qualities and try to patch the hole in our wholeness. This counter-projection can result in a syndrome known as *folie à deux*, or the "madness of two." This accounts for the "just-us-against-the-world" mentality. Any psychological deviation of one is condoned and reinforced in the other in a spiraling move away from consensus reality into isolation. The delusion is usually within the realm of possibility and often is based on past common experience. Their ability to deal with reality is undermined in favor of an escape into romantic fantasy and self-justification. This is much easier for weak egos. Mutual projection is also the basis for personality cults, but the roles are simply switched to teacher and disciple as Platonic lovers. There is an unconscious fascination, an enchantment, which comes from seeing yourself reflected in your beloved, whether it is true or not.

Another example of this fascination or *participation mystique* is the creation of talismans. Talismans are objects that you invest with seemingly magical powers to influence a situation. This is the basis of sympathetic magic. It accounts for the recent fad of using crystals as healing stones. It is fine if you use them to focus your creative imagination, but don't mistake the fact that it is your own investment of energy that brings the transformations rather than any inherent quality in the crystal. Belief systems perpetuate a mystery feeling that can lead to illusory convictions concerning "the way things work."

Another popular illusion is the concept of soul-mates or twin-flames. It is a very compelling romance to feel you are linked to your beloved through eternity. In fact, it is true, that the soul-mate can be found. However, it is once again the archetype of the inner mate that calls for your fidelity. The inner mate responds to your positive attention. And you can purposefully further this relationship by allowing time to dialogue with your *anima* or *animus*. You should write down your experience, letting it flow freely, asking and answering questions. Also, be aware of your feeling responses. When new information or other points of view emerge there is an authentic exchange. Continue as often and long as you like. But don't neglect your human relationships. Remember, you are balancing the opposites.

As your fascinations dissolve, your individual attitudes and reactions to situations become freer and more objective. Your projected contents "return" to their proper home in your psyche. You can then perceive them as psychological reality instead of seeing them "out there" in the physical world as "the neighbor I despise" (*shadow*), "that flashy new car that will bring me status" (*persona*), or "my Prince Charming" (*animus*). You are no longer at the mercy of the actions and moods of another person. You realize the source of feeling exists within yourself.

"A wolf and the dog are in the land"

PLATE 5

Alexander writes openly from Persia
That *a wolf and a dog are in the land.*
The Wise show us
That they have a common origin.

Yet the wolf comes from the east,
While the dog springs from the west.

Both are full of jealousy;
Furious, in madness, and rage,
They kill each other.

And from them comes a great poison.

When they are brought back to life,
They are indeed joined together.
From them comes the highest Medicine and best Remedy
That may be found on earth.

It has refreshed and restored the Wise,
Who honor, thank, and praise God for it.

A wolf and a dog each other constrain,
Yet in the end only one shall remain.

The Body is mortified and rendered white,
Then joined with Soul and Spirit by saturation.

"The wolf and the dog are in the land."

Chapter 5: The Adversary

Solutio

THE last plate of the lions in the valley depicted an attempt at
unification of the Spirit and Soul in the body. But the struggle for this
achievement is not over yet. However, we saw how a woman's *animus*
functions as the active representative of the spirit, or logos principle, and
gives her self-confidence. We also learned how a man's *anima* teaches him
how to reconnect with feelings and deepen intimacy. Those are external
effects of resources that need to be applied inwardly.

Once your personal projections around the inner mate are brought to
awareness, you may also become aware of their transpersonal nature. It is
the nature of all symbols of the Self to carry both a personal and transpersonal
aspect. The personal qualities relate to your personality and daily life, while
the transpersonal images have spiritual value. The transcendent *anima*
appears in her mythic forms as the Great Goddess, Great Mother, wise
Sophia, holy Virgin Mary, sacred Isis, cosmic Shakti, or a high priestess,
shamaness, or prophetess. The spiritual aspects of the *animus* can be
projected as a master of wisdom, magician, wizard, priest, teacher, shaman,
or protector.

When you do not project these images outwardly, the psychic energy they
embody is freed up for further growth. As you build your conscious
relationship with your inner mate you are engaged in a spiritual practice.
Your inner mate will then guide you into the deeper layers of your
unconscious. As you honor this process the goals of your ego and Self are
beginning to harmonize. Then you begin experiencing a functional unification of soul and spirit, or mental union of opposites. The "battle of the
sexes" is no longer waged in your psyche; instead there is a union or sacred
marriage between your feminine and masculine aspects. This takes commitment on your part, which must persist through the disturbances to your
personality and mental life.

In the process of individuation, there are three basic reasons you learn to
use these projections as "operatives":

1) to gain communion with your inner mate and access the opposite
sex resources it holds;
2) to free yourself of your subjective distortions about others so you

can develop a real relationship with them; and

3) to strengthen the link between your conscious and unconscious so you can realize your deep Self more fully.

There is an ancient Roman saying that "man is a wolf to man." In plate 5, the wolf represents Spirit manifesting through Soul, and the dog is the Body or Matter. The Body, with its instinctual nature, is now an active participant in the transformation process, not simply in the background. At this stage, in the fight to the death, the Body is mortified. This continues the process of dying to the old condition and may leave a sense of void within. Your ego experiences its subjective realm in the body as a vast, empty expanse. This sense of void only disappears after the original repression of the unconscious opens, and your ego finds that the realm within is alive with energy. But there are further trials and crises to face before the resurrection, or "bringing back to life."

The Body is rendered white and joined with Soul and Spirit by being saturated with them. *Solutio*, dissolving a solid into a liquid form, is the operation for this stage. It is a prerequisite for rebirth, a return to the womb. All your fixed attitudes and adjustment patterns must be dissolved in both mind and body before you proceed. It is an alchemical dictum that only that which has been first adequately separated can be joined. Each element of psychic life, both physical and mental, must be reduced to its original condition of *prima materia* to be useful in the alchemical process.

The first phase of the alchemical process involves coming into awareness of the heights and depths of your character. *Solutio* heralds another crisis where the contents of the deep subconscious erupt from below and overwhelm both body and mind. This sets up a long conflict which only abates when your ego stops resisting.

True, the deep self is a source of regeneration, wisdom, and nourishment, but only after you have weathered the storm resulting from exposure to all the formerly repressed inner forces. Furthermore, there is no guarantee your ego will survive this onslaught. Not everyone is heroic enough and properly equipped to make this arduous journey. So caution is the watchword. In this state, another inner form of *participation mystique* comes into play. You are held in thrall, fascinated, even hypnotized by the powerful images and forces welling up from below. You not only experience high anxiety because you are powerless, but your ego may suffer a deep psychic wound because it is stripped of its defenses.

Anxiety may change into dread. You are in dire straits, plagued by feelings of doom and gloom. Dread is the feeling of being overawed and frozen in your tracks by ominous forces. Chills go up and down your back, and your body hair bristles and raises on end. There is a sense of the uncanny, the world seems strange and surreal, and you are entranced by the hypnotically fascinating effect of the subconscious, as if in a dream. This is merely a natural product of your estrangement from the inner power. You see it as other, alien, even sinister. It surely *is* threatening. But here is a resurgence in energy from within, and it is fascinating enough to renew your interest in life. You are haunted by the notion that there is surely more beyond this condition.

Your dreams, belief system, and waking images will reflect the crisis within. The most typical are images of cataclysm and apocalypse, death and destruction. The main theme is being seized by the forces of darkness, which heralds the end of the world. It is the end of the world as you have known it. So you experience images of falling or crashing, being sucked under or downward. Natural disasters are used metaphorically, hence powerful pictures of earthquakes, volcanic eruptions, stormy weather, and flooding are common. Wild beasts are running amok, and a great clash with the power of evil seems unavoidable. The Self is perceived as an overwhelming Adversary, full of spite and venom.

Why does the Self appear as evil incarnate? Because the polarities of good and evil are intrinsic to human life. So, wherever good is found, evil must necessarily be present. The brilliant light casts a long, dark shadow. Your self-realization also includes evil, since it is a dynamic part of the primal creative source. You cannot destroy evil, even in your own life, but you can rein it in. This is a courageous moral task for the ego, which requires sacrifice. Thus, even evil can be an agent of the highest good. The Adversary is the harbinger of *solutio*.

Stripped of your defenses, you are set upon by powerful forces from within. This may mean a severe disruption of your personality. You seem overrun with irrational fears, superstitions, paranoia, and phobias. Even normal emotions, like stress, embarrassment, and excitement seem so amplified that you are overwhelmed. All your habit patterns are disturbed, and you feel very out of control. The stress comes from the uprising power of your deep Self pressing from within. Your mind is difficult to focus on task. So much energy is coming from your psyche that you are entranced. Your thought processes range from fuzzy, to stubborn, to wildly unruly. Your overstimulated mind is as befuddled as your emotional nature. It is not easily guided at this point, and mental detachment is difficult to achieve.

The ego is used to being active in the world. It is a shock when it is transfixed, open and passive, and all the primitive, raw material of the unconscious is downloaded into it. Insight is there, yes; but, it is awesome and frightening. Perhaps the only defense is for the mind to space-out into some sort of void, mentally suspended in limbo between onslaughts. This awakened intuition brings a flood of fearsome and forbidden images into awareness. It may seem like a diabolical torture, because these wrathful visions are vivid hallucinations.

If you experience this, you feel as if you are going insane. In fact, this is the same imagery the mentally ill experience, but they are unable to weather the storm. You may, at this point, be seriously deranged at times. You may oscillate between frenzy and voiding out. Your mental darkness and blankness may feel like a psychic black hole, pulling you into a pit away from daily life.

The wolf and dog are brought back to life and join each other, and in the end only one remains. The flow of dynamic energy from the deep Self reawakens and activates your body and also that portion of the unconscious that the body carries. These body memories include armoring and traumas locked into your posture and musculature. This "resurrection" of the body can produce bizarre physical symptoms of unstressing. The blocks, tensions, and constrictions that have impeded the Self in the body are being torn asunder.

This frees you to feel a sensuousness you may never have connected with before, but feels foreign, because your ego is still disenfranchised from your body. Only when the reborn ego can identify once again with your body, do you experience that vivifying sense of reunion. In the meantime, your sensitized body may revel in sensuous delights, much to the dismay of your disembodied mind. This hypersensitivity will pass in time, but in the meanwhile you may seek the sanctuary of a retreat or low-stimulus environment.

This phase opens into the mythical or religious dimension of moral and ethical behavior. Through your contact with collective evil, and the reawakened instinctual sensual urges of your body, you should be developing your own ethical stance. Your personal confrontation with the Self, as good and evil, includes the physical, emotional, mental, and spiritual spheres of existence. Sigmund Freud termed the transpersonal morality the superego. Acute awareness of your sexual and aggressive instincts, complete with explicit imagery and urges, may be very distressing.

For the spiritual aspirant, it may seem that for every step forward there are two steps backward. This confusion in regard to your normal appetites may create an approach-avoidance polarization. Trying to be holy, you may swing from chastity to hedonistic abandon. But, spirituality and instinctuality go hand-in-hand as you move toward wholeness. Your mind must bear and resolve the conflict. As you open yourself to the magnetic upward pull of spirit, you are also subjected to the lower urges of the instincts. This anguish is an intense moral dilemma for some, but it is the price of integration of all your human resources.

When your mental ego is devoured by the hungry desirousness symbolized by the wolf, you experience the religious crisis in which your old ruling ideas have lost their meaning. You realize that you have been missing a lot of the universal aspects in your appraisal of reality. But the shame and humiliation of your shortcomings and oversights is mixed with the pleasure of discovery and connection with your depths. This union of opposites may produce more ambivalence. Your ego's task here is not really to build moral strength, but to comprehend the reality of the inner world. You come to understand truly that imagination is reality, and your ego's control fantasies are really undermined.

In *solutio*, you unite the powers of above and below. You integrate the higher spiritual powers with your personal experience, grounding them in day-to-day reality. This produces the paradoxical poison-panacea. The solvent distills the poison through the alchemical art. This art is analysis and requires your thorough examination of the problematic situation. This essence is poisonous if you succumb to the deadly danger of embroilment in worldly affairs to the exclusion of the Great Work. If your ego acknowledges the Self as its new center of gravity, your personality begins healing, meaning is restored to life, and you operate from a solid system of values. This is the panacea that harmonizes the realms of spiritual and conjugal love. The Self replaces your ego as the new center of your personality.

Solutio obviously is an irrational process. It derives from meditation on the objective products spontaneously arising from your depths, like dreams and fantasies. In this way it unites your awareness with contents from an essentially unconscious process. This meditation is an objective way of conducting your self-introspection. In taking stock of yourself, you become aware of your projections and how they falsify the nature of your experience. Projections pull you into the poisonous worldly entanglements. By looking within, overcoming this tendency, you come to a degree of self-knowledge and understanding that divinity truly lies within you. The main resistance to this is your tendency to get actively engrossed in external reality through your senses.

As long as this outward tendency undermines your inner quest, your soul is tortured and suffers spiritual martyrdom. There is anguish over neglecting your spiritual side. You are again in despair over your process of transformation, but it is the torment that comes from unlimited affection. You suffer mental torment from being confronted with the overwhelming nature of unlimited possibilities.

This is awesome and frightening to your ego. But, according to the illustration of the wolf and the dog, your ego should be able to channel these emotions, just as the river in the channel flows placidly through the town. It does not encroach as a raging flood. Rather the body of water in the background remains in its proper confines. It serves the town (cultural values), rather than threatening it. The bridge between the opposing banks remains intact.

If you are attached to a one-sided attitude, you can dissolve it by developing a more comprehensive viewpoint. *Solutio* is the dissolution of your old attitude and may be experienced as a threat to the worldview of your ego. Your ego is invested in maintaining its control fantasies. It tends to assume that it knows "where it's at" and builds your personality from its perception of order. Your ego embraces a paradigm or overview of reality, usually called your worldview.

Should you find yourself around someone with a more convincing or comprehensive worldview, it can wash away the solid ground from under your feet. This is not always welcomed news, even though it may be an improvement and more reality-oriented than your previous attitudes. As the solid bottom washes out from your world, you feel adrift until you can make the adjustments and assimilate what you have learned about life and existence.

The agents of *solutio* can be internal or external. When you perceive someone as knowing more than yourself, you can project the archetypes of the "Wise Old Man" or "Wise Old Woman" onto them, regardless of their age. Watch for the delusion! Some of these individuals may be wise teachers, philosophers, or saintly role models; others may seek to trick you deliberately, or be deluding themselves. Perhaps they do know more than you, but they can't possibly embody the omniscience of your own inner wisdom figure. You always have the choice of embracing or rejecting their broader view.

The long-range aim of *solutio* is the unification of the opposites represented here by the wolf and the dog. The wolf is masculine in nature, the dog feminine. Both archetypal elements are being dissolved and united simultaneously. In terms of therapy, this means that individuation is a two-way movement of separating or distinguishing, and coming together or integration. In self-analysis you distinguish archetypes from your personal experience, then integrate them into your physical reality. They are no longer mental abstractions, but living psychic realities to you. You experience a vital connection with your shadow and *anima/animus*.

The forces of the deeper subconscious must also be subjected to this process of differentiation and reintegration. This formula is known in alchemy as *Solve et Coagula*. It symbolizes the axiom "that which has not been separated cannot be joined." There is a conflict of wild and domesticated energies before their unification.

There is a famous magical illustration of the figure Baphomet in the work of nineteenth-century French magus, Eliphas Levi. This figure is usually misconstrued by the uninitiated as being the Devil. It is actually a complex symbol of integration, and a good example of the Adversary. On its arms are inscribed *solve* and *coagula*. The upward pointing arm is *solve*. The downward-pointing arm says *coagula*, and indicates a move into manifestation. The figure is an integration of masculine and feminine traits, human and bestial, earthy and psychic, good and evil. Between its horns sprouts a brilliant torch as the symbol of divine revelation.

The conflict between the wild wolf and domesticated dog is the antagonism between lust and love. Both are agents of *solutio*. Their union symbolizes the healing of the split between physical and spiritual soul-images. Outwardly for men, this could manifest as an end to a madonna-whore complex, and an ability to find one woman both sexy and spiritually inspiring. Uniting your wild life-force (libido) with devotion in love can dissolve many problems or blockages to your further transformation. This is one reason spiritual teachers usually recommend monogamy.

The best qualities of your ego will survive *solutio*, especially your tendency toward spiritual devotion. You will be reformed, but still be yourself after the regression in the service of transcendence. The pain of dissolution and dismemberment, the awe and dread of exposure to the broader reality, all lead to immersion in the healing creative energy flow, which is like a spiritual baptism. Your old rigid attitudes become much softer. You have been through a grueling purification ordeal, but finally begin finding solutions to your problems.

You may even find new meaning in the faith of your youth at this point. If orthodox religion is not effective for you, your intuition and faith may lead you to the mythic dimension or a metaphorical perspective on life. Myths only become living realities for you as you experience their dynamics in your personal life. Learning about archetypal powers gives you insight, but is ineffective at influencing your behavior unless it is backed by experience.

To gain this firsthand knowledge, you must become like an alchemist's apprentice, learning the technique, and practicing it diligently. You must keep an eye on your dreams and fantasies, which used to seem so worthless to you. Gradually, the light of understanding will dawn. Be sure to enter your inner dramas, or waking dreams, with your authentic personality, complete with your ethical stance. By watching your imagination critically, you avoid flitting off into meaningless daydreams.

By morally evaluating your position in both internal and external reality, and harmonizing them, your insights start to become real. You must consider what your images mean to you personally and not merely observe them like a movie. You need to understand their meaning, value it, and apply it (coagula). If you integrate your lessons into daily life, the Self is revealed in matter. Your physical equivalent of the deep Self takes shape as you are transformed.

Your moral insight develops as you struggle with the shadow and the Adversary. When you are unconscious of your deep creative process, many resources remain latent. But you can develop more ethical consciousness as you withdraw your projections and interiorize them.

With this comes the realization of a center of insight which looks beyond crime, illness, pathology, and therapy to deeper reality. You can have a perception of "sin," but without the guilt, accusal, and punishment which come from compulsively acting it out. Originally "sin" was an archery term for "missing the mark." You might ask yourself where you are missing your own personal mark, or goal in your life. When you are connecting with intense moral awareness, you realize evil is a necessary component of the universe and notice when it presents itself to your awareness as a moral and ethical problem.

In solutio, the regression of your psychic energy may be experienced as guilt and remorse. For some, it is an insoluble problem that stops them dead in their tracks, while for others it spurs the quest for truth.

"A poisonous dragon inhabits the forest"

PLATE 6

A poisonous Dragon inhabits the forest,
Yet lacks nothing:
When he sees the Sun and its fire,
He scatters his poison and flies upward fiercely;

Neither can the Basilisk master him,
For the Dragon knows well how to kill this serpent.

It struggles with all and yet is nothing.

His color increases with death,
And from his venom can be made Medicine.

He consumes the poison completely,
Devouring his envenomed tail.

This consumed,
The noblest Balm comes from within himself,
Providing the gift of Youth.

This greatly pleases all the Wise.

This surely is a great marvel and wonder,
When the best Balm flows from the Dragon's ill.

Mercury, precipitated and sublimated properly by chemistry, is dissolved in his own water and recoagulated.

Chapter 6: Great Mother

Coagulatio

THE pose of the dragon makes the Uroborous symbol, a creature forming a circle as it bites its own tail. This is an image which reflects our original primal fusion with the maternal realm of the Great Mother, or Mother Nature. *Coagulatio* has to do with grounding, and the unconscious as Great Mother is the primal, instinctual ground from which our individual awareness emerges. Your ego gained its escape from this primitive state of immersion by disidentifying with the body and withstanding the regressive pull into unconsciousness.

Now, once again, your ego is challenged to a higher order of unity with your body, mind, and emotions. To accomplish this, the ego must die and this dragon symbolizes the paradox of death/rebirth as it devours its own envenomed tail. It heralds the impending doom of the ego and only hints at the mysterious prospect of regeneration. Your ego must voluntarily expose itself to the annihilating force of the Mother Dragon and pass through the gates of death without being destroyed. Through ego-death, your ego ultimately reconstitutes itself, intact and functional, but you no longer identify exclusively with it. Even so, you experience intense separation anxiety as you disidentify and your sense of self transcends mere ego.

To create this higher-order self means dissolving the blocks and barriers between your mind and body. These blocks are ways you have learned to hold on or hold in strong instincts and urges that are socially taboo. Flesh, sin, and suffering are not synonymous, but because life in the body can be a source of excruciating pain, we learn to dissociate from it, and this cuts us off from pleasures as well. We have fallen into the habit of thinking about our body parts, rather than giving them feeling-attention. Tension is simply muscular pressure built up by holding in taboo feelings or impulses. These blocks were initially protective for our emerging sense of self, but now just represent resistance to feeling particular emotions.

These buried feelings need to be released, so you can find a harmony between the involuntary forces of nature at work within you, and your human voluntary intention. When you can connect your entire psychophysical being, you are finally free to live life, in the now, without the primal fear of death holding you back. Ego-death allows you to reconcile your being with your mortality. Mystics, in fact, encourage us to "die daily" in meditation, returning to the inner world each day. By reconnecting with the ground of consciousness you gain the "courage to be," but it may feel too intense and overwhelming. For the ego, it feels like losing control, but the broader truth is that the ego simply relinquishes its control fantasy; in reality, its will never was dominant over the unconscious.

Shame is the primary emotion relating to this state, as you face your human limitations. It is fundamental to being human, as related in the story of Adam and Eve. They "knew shame" immediately upon gaining a self-reflective consciousness. Shame is natural and healthy, but toxic shame—shame over your essential being, or viewing yourself as a defective human being—is unhealthy. Before you commit an act shame appears to you as discretion; after the fact shame is experienced as disgrace.

Healthy shame is a natural impulse to modesty and privacy. But shame as disgrace means premature exposure and it is painful, unexpected, and disorienting. The suffering creates not just a shattering effect, but also the psychic heat necessary for transformation. Painful self-consciousness can lead to self-discovery, an intimate relationship with yourself. This confirms and enlarges your identity, creating a new perspective.

Healthy shame keeps you grounded by keeping you aware of your human limitations, providing boundaries and structure. It gives you permission to be human. It establishes a balance between "holding on" and "letting go." As an emotion, it expresses your legitimate need for privacy. Toxic shame is not an emotion, but has become a state of being.

The function of shame is to preserve wholeness, integrity, and dignity in respect to such instinctual processes as sexuality, elimination, suffering, and dying. Bodily functions are rarely only physiological and that is why we surround them with taboos, symbols, and meanings. These barriers safeguard our human experience. Obscenity is a deliberate violation of the sense of shame. Shame only restricts defiling exposure, not all exposure.

Shamelessness is unlimited self-assertion. When we are shameless, we are vulnerable and liable to hurt others as well. Shame protects the human meaning, or sacred quality of sexuality. The ancient Greeks had a word for shame as it relates to sexuality, *aidos*, denoting the "awe" and mystery of this libidinous force. Shamelessness denudes the body of her mysteries. Shame can be viewed as the conscience of love, creating discernment. It allows us to engage in intimacy without invasively crossing another's boundaries. Shame inhibits the sexual urge until your whole self can respond to the entire being of another.

This plate represents the potentiality for re-owning your body in consciousness, so you experience yourself as a total psychosomatic being. You are, in fact, a unified organism. There is no mind/body dichotomy in nature. Separation from the body is a defense by a damaged, weak, or immature ego. Your heightened sensory experience is simply accomplished by flowing with your ongoing psychophysiological process, and identifying with that natural wisdom coupled with your individual purpose and goals. But before this is possible, you must once again encounter that old dragon who encompasses the heights and depths of awareness, and contains all the virtues and defects of mankind.

The dragon represents the *Anima Mundi*, or Soul of the World, which is the sum-total of planetary existence. She is the animating force behind all events, images, and material forms. She presents us with an awesome pandemonium of images, and your ego must this time not fight its way free, but surrender to forces that cross your subjective will, and come into a new relationship with the collective unconscious. The mystery images of the psyche are the compelling source of both morality and spirituality.

To experience psychic reality means to be in soul, in the realm of the imagination, as if interacting with its inhabitants and locales. Approach your images with a loving attentiveness, an attitude of service. The original connotation of *therapy* meant "service to the gods," and this process goes on within when you relate to the patterns playing through you. Your inner visionary experience, be it wrathful or beatific, is an expression of your soul. Through images, the unconscious profoundly affects your worldview, your health, and your relationships. Your future spirituality is contained within your immediate experience of being in soul. Soul is the middle world between gross materiality and the spiritual world.

This dragon represents the reopening of the interaction between the ego and the Great Mother archetype, the maternal realm of nature, body, and instinct. It is the ground of consciousness. However, in this renewing of relations with the maternal principle, your ego is confronted with its negative aspect, the dark, instinctual Terrible Mother. This awesome feminine force is not conditioned by your original, personal experience of mothering. This is Goddess, in pure form, as an inner, psychic, spiritual reality.

In her animal form, she appears here as one of the great beasts of the unconscious, the Dragon. Her personified forms are dark and rude, like wicked witch or whore. Her elemental forms include raging waters, fires, and winds. Like the Hindu goddess Kali, she is lustful and bloodthirsty; her name is Desire. This forest of darkness has the power to annihilate the puny ego; at best it will feel lost in the abyss of the transcendent imagination. All its efforts to resist this ominous force only seem to add to her strength.

When your ego yields its combative position, you stop hurting yourself unnecessarily. The Great Mother only appears adversarial when your ego is alienated from her.

If the ego gives up its dragon-slaying role and takes the plunge of faith further into the depths, spiritual rebirth may be found. By surrendering, your instincts are pacified, and the Terrible Mother transforms herself into an inspirational goddess full of love, light, and wisdom. But she is not subdued easily, and there will be repeated episodes of temptation by this dark and strong power, whose magnetic draw into the deep abyss is seemingly irresistible. The aim is to once and for all dissolve and disintegrate your old ego until there is no return to the old condition. This is a risky point on the path, and some egos are simply destroyed by this regressive pull. Mystics find a way out of this madmen's hell and keep their heads afloat in the ocean of the unconscious.

Thus, at its worst, the *Anima Mundi* personifies all the ignorance, folly, hatred and other negative thoughts created by mankind throughout aeons. Eliphas Levi described it as "the Old Queen of the world ... Every uncurbed passion, every selfish pleasure, every licentious energy of humanity." Her benevolent aspects likewise combine the sum total of the virtue and heroism of the human species. Negative characterizations of her include the Beast of the Apocalypse and the Great Whore of Babylon.

The monster of the deep symbolizes the forces of chaos, especially evil passions, paganism, and the oppressive powers of the world. Yet, this beast within us guards the treasure of the unconscious, which is so difficult to attain. The *Anima Mundi* fascinates but does not obliterate the ego of the mystic. The strong, heroic ego passes the trial or ordeal, and is in fact stimulated by the intense provocation. Even this "deadly" *anima* can have a growth-promoting effect, most likely through spontaneous, transformative visions.

The Uroborous dragon has a relationship to the astrological and mythical Saturn. Saturn is the maker and breaker of forms, lord of time and manifestation. In mythology, Saturn devoured his own children. In the same way all physical forms have only a limited life before they change form. The dragon is also a symbol of time, for the evolution of Earth is determined by time. We know only too well that we ourselves are bound by time and by the form of the body.

For each one of us the dragon is the constant treadmill of mundane life, good or bad, depending on the conditions we have created by the unique attitude of mind which is our individual responsibility. Psychologically, the dragon exists within each one of us as that wild, powerful mythological beast. In this respect, it represents your consciousness of the material world and your attitude towards it.

In the text, the dragon sees the sun, scatters poison, and flies off fiercely. It has an aspect that opposes the sun, which is the center and main support of our earthly and spiritual existence, and symbolizes Spirit. Your personality and material body tend to be repelled by the action of the Spirit. The action of the Spirit is often to open new avenues and close down well-trodden paths, much to the dismay of the personality and its desires. One of the worst side effects of spiritual activation is that once the blocks are removed, Spirit operates within you much more efficiently. But, if your personality and lifestyle are out of balance, the manifestation of your newly found power tends to be distorted.

The immediate effect of an initiatory experience may result in a revised attitude to life, but character failings are more obvious than ever before. The brighter the light you shine in your dark corners, the more debris you are likely to find. Aspirants to the spiritual life are often impatient and stubborn. Inpouring spiritual voltage tends to amplify whatever characteristics are native to your personality, and you can expect some negative consequences. Again, balance and equilibrium are the keywords, and the tests of these are serenity, consistency, and adaptability in the life of the aspirant.

The "scattered poison" in the text refers to the deviations in the personality. The poison which prevents right relationship with the universe is a wrong attitude to it. The collective personal flaws of humanity eventually lead to wars, atrocities, and other destruction. But this breakdown can be used so that a nobler world rises from the ashes of the old. You cannot condone unbalanced force in the world, but many times you lack the long-range perspective that can see destruction as a necessary part of the growth process.

Coagulatio means to congeal, or become more solid or earthy. Your ego cannot soar unfettered by physical existence into its spiritual fantasies. To move toward wholeness, you must balance your aspiration with your personal concrete reality. However, by gaining awareness of the archetypal process operating within, you can actually enlarge your experience of concrete reality to include the realm of the psyche. Consciousness of your inner dynamics, knowledge of your own evil, and insightful relationships all demonstrate the process of *coagulatio* at work.

You can only realize and integrate archetypes when you experience them in literal, personalized forms. Then you can have meaningful, internal relationships with them in concrete forms. For each individual they are unique, but they share primary characteristics. For example, the parental archetypes are rooted in your childhood experience of your caregivers, but their own personalities get in the way of direct archetypal expression. Thus, most frequently, archetypes are earthed in limited or distorted forms.

By exploring the imaginal aspects of your inner and outer relationships, you ground and "materialize" archetypal forces. They augment your personal life rather than simply raging through you. These descents of the archetype into concrete forms are a way you can personally encounter the divine. You simply become conscious of them and learn to "see" that which previously had no form. Your ego has a defined relationship with them, rather than merely perceiving them as qualities or concepts. Psychologically, this is the union of ordinary human reality and the transpersonal Self. *Coagulatio* thus becomes a dialogue with events, situations, and circumstances.

The dragon is an early stage of the original untransformed substance, manifesting as passion or desire. If you already have strong desires, you don't need to spend much time on this operation. It is for those who are not hedonistic by lifestyle. What is required at this stage of the Great Work is your active, responsive ego participation. The sun, which the dragon sees, is the masculine aspect of consciousness: the ego incarnated in pride and desire. You must invest energy into your transformation process. The motivating factor is either impulse, compulsion, or will. In any event, desire promotes *coagulatio*.

When your psychic energy is mobilized as desire, you participate in all aspects of life more fully, and experience the sweetness of fulfillment by taking calculated risks. But fulfillment implies a limit or boundary condition. *Coagulatio* thus symbolizes the limitations of your personal reality, karma or destiny. It brings shame, and perhaps guilt since mistakes are bound to happen in being human. But it can also bring redemption, as your tribulation gives way to transcendence.

The text speaks of noble balm, an elixir of youth. This spiritual food of immortality signifies the ability of your conscious ego to assimilate the previously unconscious contents of the Self. So, if you are ever offered food in a fantasy or dream, always eat it, even if it seems unpleasant like strong medicine. This image of an immortal body, the ultimate *coagulatio* of the spirit, is a boundary condition with profound possibilities. It is the equivalent of the alchemical symbol known as the Philosopher's Stone, the prime symbol of individuation.

Within this dragon lies its own healing power. Your ego's desirousness, especially for spiritual growth, can be transformed into your incarnating

Self. When you actively participate in transformative therapy, you solidify your personality. *Coagulatio* symbolizes the process of ego formation and transformation. If you can become fully connected to the Self, your goal of individuation is accomplished. Assimilating your psychological complexes helps this along.

Any complex reflects the unconscious interaction of an archetype in your personal life. When it is conscious, the complex, which is an aspect of the subconscious (subpersonality), is elevated and becomes a positive influence instead of a negative one. It transforms into its more spiritual aspects. In other words, it is *perceived* differently. But your ego can only tolerate small doses of this potent medicine. In dreams, *coagulatio* may appear as things falling or "coming down to earth" like airplanes, bodies, rocks, etc.

Coagulatio is also linked to the moon and matriarchal consciousness. The Great Mother expresses cyclic time, much like the Wise Old Man relates to linear development. Whether she is known as the White Goddess, Great Mother, or virgin Isis, she is the symbol of the archetypal Feminine. Ancient matriarchal agricultural groups saw her quality reflected in the moon. All the later goddesses of the Greek pantheon are contained in this universal symbol of the Earth Mother.

Classically, the goddess is associated with the vegetation cycle of death/ rebirth so typical of agricultural life. She rules the domestic arena as well as nature. Her primary characteristic is fertility. This fertility extends to the fecundity of imagination. You can plant the seeds of change in the fertile soil of your creative imagination. Then, to the extent that you nourish those seeds, they will flower and bear fruit in your behavior, body, emotions, and thoughts.

The feminine goddess is single in essence but displays a multitude of forms. Her mythic cults enacted mysteries of death and revival. They celebrated the immortality of the mother-daughter relationship. The goddess embodies all contrasts: she is light and dark, life and death, beginning and end. This Great Mother is the matrix of all manifestation perceivable by humans. The whole life of mankind is governed by the goddess, mother of all-that-exists. Her worship is still with us today both in the cult of the Virgin Mary and the neopagan revival.

Even though matriarchal consciousness characterizes the spiritual nature of woman, it also manifests in men who allow their *anima* consciousness, or inner femininity, to come to the fore. The goddess reveals herself in creative inspiration, the hunches of instinct and intuition, and the raw energy of life itself. It is a distinct advantage for men to establish a harmony with the moon power. She counsels meditation, contemplation, waiting and watching, dreaming, and remembering.

Matriarchal consciousness focuses around growth and transformation. In this mode understanding appears as if it were a "conception," and the metaphors of pregnancy and birth are common. The knowledge revealed by the goddess is not one of learned or demonstrated truths, but a firsthand experience of transformation. She encourages direct, intimate participation. When your rational, over-achieving ego-centered awareness has burnt out, your quiet, reflective lunar consciousness emerges to cool the fires of the spirit. The feminine image holds the keys to experience of the inner planes for both men and women. She rules the transformative mysteries of initiation.

As a bestower of initiation, the goddess progressively educates your emotional nature. Alchemical training of your image-making faculty is the beginning of a new way of using your mind. You may become self-initiated into the Moon mysteries through careful attention to the stirring of subconscious memories. A personal relationship to the goddess brings far more understanding of life than you can ever hope to achieve by the mere study of psychology. By respecting the image of the goddess within, and honoring your personification of her as the prime representative of your soul, you create a magical link between your daily consciousness and the subtle matter of the Great Mother's soul.

The dual nature of the goddess is shown by her two characters—Good and Terrible Mother. Her elementary nature has both a positive and a negative pole. She is pictured as either an all-embracing protectress or as the devouring Terrible Mother. Her transformative nature also carries good and bad imagery. She not only governs cyclic rebirth and inspiration, but also the mysteries of intoxication, madness, and death. Her negative traits are symbolized by the dark New Moon; positive aspects by the Full Moon.

She compels us to touch upon the depths of our own emotional intensity. Her mysteries reveal a timeless realm akin to the experience of immortality. The supreme inspiration of the feminine appears now as the Wise Old Woman. Her cyclic aspects include Virgin, Mother, and Crone. This divine being is the symbol of the Feminine Self, core of all being.

"Two birds lie within the nest"

PLATE 7

There is a nest you may find in the forest,
Where Hermes' bird keeps her brood;

One wants to fly upward,
The other lies still in the nest.

Yet neither will leave the other;
The one below clings to the one above.

In this way they stay together,
Like a man at home with his wife,
Submitting to the discipline
Of the most harmonious union
At all times.

So it is sealed permanently
Under the rulership of God the Father.

Two birds lie within the nest
Yet become one when finally at rest.

Mercury, being sublimated often, is at length fixed so that it can no longer fly away and escape through the action of fire. The sublimation is repeated often until it becomes fixed.

"Two birds lie within the nest."

Chapter 7: Wise Old Man

Sublimatio

THESE two birds in the woods depict the continuing conflict between spirit and body. The bird of Hermes is the Phoenix, symbol of regeneration or rebirth. In Egypt, it was known as the *bennu* bird. The priests of Heliopolis alleged the phoenix arrived renewed from Arabia every 500 years. Heliopolis was the city of the Sun, and this bird is a spiritual missionary.

The *bennu* bird was the prototype of the individual soul, and Hermes, the Egyptian Thoth, is the lord of magic and transformation. The pursuit of depth psychology is a Hermetic process, as is alchemy. The self-reviving qualities of this bird mirror those of the spiritual soul. The arrival of this heavenly emissary heralds the favor of the divine power. Its qualities include virtue, righteousness, sincerity, and integrity.

As one of the elemental operations, *sublimatio* is associated with the element air. To sublimate means to elevate or transmute to a higher form, and air is the medium through which this process occurs. Therefore, *sublimatio* psychologically denotes the raising to consciousness of formerly unconscious contents. It has an ennobling effect. The alchemical task of this phase is to sublimate, or purify, the body and coagulate, or incarnate the spirit.

One of the primary qualities of this stage is responsibility. Flights into the spiritual heights can have an escapist quality if undertaken at the wrong time or for the wrong reason. In this case they are most likely to degenerate into mere daydreams or wishful thinking. Watch yourself carefully if you find you develop rationalizations for eluding the hassles of daily life. Even the devout and well-intentioned mystic can develop evasive patterns at certain junctures.

Evasion on the physical level means inertia or laziness; mentally and emotionally it comes as pride and hypocrisy. With awareness of archetypal forces, you develop a different relationship to responsibility and integrity. It takes time for the ego to adjust. Consciousness may soar to the heights for a time, then returns to the security of the nest. So examine the motives for even your spiritual pursuits with philosophical detachment.

The process of differentiation (*solutio*) and integration (*coagulatio*) must be repeated over and over again. Then the two birds in the forest will become one. Inner life is directed to the spirit and outer life to the material world. Meditation, discernment, and discrimination elevate consciousness when the spirit within desires to drop its identification with matter. But matter has a way of attracting spirit back to it, because without Spirit, matter has neither purpose nor meaning.

This process continues until the divine spark of your spirit fully assimilates the lessons of matter, and is purged of grossness. Each round of distillation refines you further. In meditation, your consciousness is painfully and gradually expanded by concentration and striving for right relationship with the forces of the cosmos. But the process crawls along at a snail's pace.

As the text indicates, Mercury, the Hermetic process, must be sublimed and then coagulated to slow down its movement. This slowing down is very important in the alchemical process. The spirit hidden in matter can become visible only when you are able to extract the meaning of a situation or mood. If your ego identifies with the subconscious or unconscious aspects of the Self, you get a contaminated result.

Discrimination is either lacking or cloudy; the responsibility of the ego in the process is lacking. Purification occurs through separation from this contaminated state. The spirit and soul then ascends. The body is made complete, but not perfect, by spiritualizing it.

You can adopt a viewpoint where your problems are seen from the elevated perspective of objective spirituality. Then you find some degree of release from your merely personal view. You come to understand that the ups and downs of life have a transcendent meaning that was not apparent at first. This archetypal perspective promotes *sublimatio*. The "higher" the perspective, the "grander" the vision. The down side of this process is that the higher you go, the less effective you are at influencing what you observe. Humans have the capacity to influence the material world much more easily than the archetypal forces.

Some seek a shortcut to enlightenment and *sublimatio* by "getting high." One of the problems of insight gained with psychedelic drugs is the inability of the psychonaut to ground the lessons of the trip. To make insights practical, they must be grounded in daily life. *Sublimatio* is an extraction process. It is the process of extracting the transpersonal, objective meaning from your purely subjective, reactionary responses to life's crises. The revelations of the archetypal psyche release you from your personal ego attitudes. You can then gain a living relationship with the archetypal dimension, which was known in the past as paradise or heaven.

The descending bird represents the incarnating archetypal process. To

maintain balance, modern man needs a descent into the depths of his soul and a coagulation or earthing of spiritual values in his lifestyle. The ascending bird represents many regions of insight and spiritual power, but most individuals have access only to those most easily reached. This phase of the alchemical journey represents a *sublimatio* of a lesser sort than mystical rapture, which comes later.

We do not usually view reality from the highest ethical perspective, but more often from the perspective of expediency. But you can aspire to develop the objective detachment that a higher perspective brings. A higher view is equivalent to a broader perspective that concentrates less on minute detail and more on scope. Therefore, morality is a product of *sublimatio*, an elevation of consciousness. As the psychic value and meaning of concrete situations is extracted, a view independent of personal preferences emerges.

As individuals, we can each make a contribution to both mankind and the collective unconscious. All of our meager steps in consciousness-raising make a permanent contribution to our species. Through this process we all contribute to earthing spiritual force. There is, however, some danger of dissociation or mental illness in *sublimatio*. Contaminated operations can manifest as fantasies of abduction by aliens, or being the new messiah, or in other delusions.

To recap the death/rebirth experience: The closer the ego comes to surrendering to an enlarged, liberating experience, the more anxiety grows. The ego senses that a catastrophe of immense proportions is at hand. This destruction encompasses physical destruction, emotional breakdown, mental defeat, and moral failure. To the ego, its imminent demise seems to come from an external agent of merciless destruction.

The sense of orientation in life is dissolved, perhaps never to be regained in the worst case scenario. The cycles of ego death and rebirth continue as long as self-exploration is the imperative. This imperative can come from the will of the personality or from the irresistible action of the Self. The emphasis on different aspects of growth may change and pressures increase until this phase is completed.

Ultimately, only your paranoia concerning a pro-active approach to life is relinquished. This tentativeness about living comes from traumas experienced in the initial phases of life within the womb and during the birth experience. Birth trauma and your original confrontation with birth/ death conditions your attitudes about life and the ego's experience of the paradox of death/rebirth. A negative blueprint creates an unnatural compulsion to remain rigidly in control at all times, defensiveness, and over- or under-achievement. The *coagulatio* of ego-death is absolutely necessary for a positive rebirthing experience. The godforms of the breakdown are wrathful gods of blood, lust, and dismemberment.

Both mystic and psychedelic accounts of the visions immediately following ego-death are of radiant, supernatural light and beauty and/or entities which convey a sense of bliss, peace, and serenity. This brings a sense of spiritual liberation, even salvation. The spiritual emergency, or emergence, is over, or accomplished. The soul feels cleansed and purified. Anxiety, guilt, and depression are only vague memories, seemingly a lifetime away. Self esteem and compassion for others are enhanced, as is *joie de vivre*.

This rebirthing can be accomplished by several therapeutic and yogic techniques, most of which focus around controlled or directed use of the breath. Remember, air is the element of *sublimatio*. Air relates directly to breath, experientially. In Greek, breath is *pneuma* which translates most directly as "spirit." In Eastern systems, the equivalent is *prana*, and rhythmic breathing is used to increase the charge of spirituality in the body, and to circulate and distribute this energy so that the practitioner remains in balance. Aspiration is the spiritual quality that is enhanced through attention to the breath during meditation.

In yoga this technique of rapid breathing is called *bastrika*, the "bellows." In Kundalini yoga this breath of fire is used for arousing Kundalini energy, the coiled serpent power at the base of the spine. Its goal is to open energy blocks in the body. Breathing into each of the *chakras*, systematically, finally works the blocks out. Hyperventilating amplifies your emotional tension to a crescendo, which is followed by release, and resolution. It facilitates emotional catharsis.

There are a number of breath therapies that employ rapid breathing or hyperventilation to bring a person into closer connection with emotions. The process of rebirthing as outlined by Leonard Orr has circular breathing as its first element. It helps you come fully into the present moment and keep a balanced awareness between focusing and defocusing of attention. This enhances the process of integration when emotions come up that require working through.

Another therapeutic system, holotropic healing, is promoted by consciousness researcher Stanislav Grof, M.D. It goes past verbal therapy to a direct encounter with your birth/death and the transpersonal domain. Grof calls the therapeutic effects of intense breathing *pneumocatharsis*. Increasing the rate and depth of breathing at a natural pace loosens psychological defenses and leads to release of unconscious and superconscious material.

Deep seated blocks are discharged, thereby reducing psychosomatic tensions.

Metaphorically, sublimation is part of the process of distillation or refinement of that which is in a gross state by raising it up. Your unconscious complexes and past traumas can be raised into consciousness during *sublimatio*. This provides an opportunity for catharsis, and behavioral change. It frees up more of your energy for spiritual aspiration. And the more you connect with and ground your spirituality the more inner strength you have available for further efforts at self-realization.

In this phase of *sublimatio*, many seekers are drawn to either genuine holy men or false prophets. This desire for discipleship corresponds with an amplification of the archetype of the sublime sage, man of wisdom, or the Holy Spirit. Here your sense of responsibility and discrimination can rescue you from years of potential spiritual suicide. The inexperienced seeker may even follow a person who believes he is a sage or teacher and actively recruit disciples to further his egotistical aims.

This is the archetypal source of the current rash of personality cults. These spiritual teachers may pose as saints, but they are incapable of producing transforming experiences in their followers or themselves. The phenomena surrounding this type of teacher comes from the activation of the Wise Old Man archetype in the subconscious minds of the followers.

An even greater danger is the charismatic teacher who has some actual level of realization. In Jungian psychology, this living out of a charismatic mission is personified in the archetype of the "mana personality," one who manifests his or her personal power and can fascinate crowds with words of wisdom. These enigmatic personalities can intrigue or manipulate the masses, and history is full of the tales of these charmers. If they use their charismatic talent to exploit others, they are engaging in a form of psychic slavery. This is the exact reverse of alchemical practice, which seeks to free us from bondage. Be aware of anyone who practices the exercise of power over others against their wills.

The evolution of a false prophet as leader of his own cult is an interesting phenomena. Most are well-motivated in the beginning, unless they are simply outright con men. They have probably been the followers or even model disciples of true teachers. But they never learned to submit their wills or surrender fully to a power greater than their own egos. So, they remain on the ego level, exercising their powers and skills for self-aggrandisement, rather than using them compassionately in service.

The self-image of these false gurus is enhanced with all sorts of trappings. There is a false glamour which pervades the whole atmosphere, but the "true believer" is blind to the many signs of crass materialism. Their clothes and affectatious mannerisms are employed like props to suggest their lofty station. There are examples of this type in mainstream religion as well as the sphere of less orthodox magicians, mystics, and shamans. You may find one leading a psychological group or in a powerful position in the priesthood. All traditions have their false prophets and usurpers, for there is temptation all along the path.

If you have come in contact with a dark or fallen teacher, or been outrageously exploited, you may as well view it as a philosophical lesson. But you need not make the same mistake twice. Teachers can only take you as far as they themselves have progressed. There is no harm in following a lesser teacher until you find one who is greater, unless that teacher is self-serving and manipulative. Risk investigating a teacher thoroughly before letting him influence your belief systems. No doubt you will find many dead ends while learning something of value every step of the way. This is another form of enchantment, enmeshment, or *participation mystique* you learn to eventually see through.

If you meet a real saint, it will become apparent to you in time because the answers to your burning inner questions will be revealed. However, real teachers don't usually volunteer direction, unless specifically asked. Furthermore, they may place roadblocks in your way to test your sincerity and commitment. You will hear none of the fantastic promises or evasive allusions used to spin the web of the power hungry, self-proclaimed master of wisdom.

If you remain a serious aspirant, you will be automatically drawn to your own special teachers. In time, you develop discernment. One of the most expedient means of quickening your spirituality at this time is contact with someone who has established a solid living connection to the spiritual realm.

"A white and red bird are bound together"

PLATE 8

There is a Forest in India
Where *two birds are bound together;*
One is white, the other red.

Together they bite themselves to death,
And one completely devours the other.

Both then change into a white dove—
From the Dove will be born a Phoenix.

It must be black and strong;
From death it assumes a new life.

Such cunning and strength has God given you,
That he lives in the future and never dies,
Granting us riches and health,
So that we can do great wonders.

It is for us that the Wise have written so deeply.

See the two great birds, Matter and Spirit,
Devour each other beneath the tree.

Matter is placed afresh for digestion in horse-dung, or a warm bath.
The Air or Spirit, formerly removed from the Matter, is now poured
    over it.
Matter is made white by the operation, Spirit red by Art.
The interaction between the essences tends to perfection and
The Philosopher's Stone is prepared in this way.

"A white and red bird are bound together."

Chapter 8: Marriage of Opposites

Albedo, Rubedo, and Coniunctio

INITIALLY, the text describes further conflict experienced in the psyche between spirit and matter. The images of transformation into a dove and then a phoenix indicate the beginning of psychic renewal. The condition of psychic death yields to that of a new, higher life. Undergoing the alchemical process has allowed an unfolding of the regenerative change. The original, gross state of contamination of consciousness has been refined through a purification process leading to profound psychological and spiritual regeneration.

This process is initiated by "cooking" the raw material of psychophysical life. The means include psychological analysis, experience of nonordinary states of consciousness in guided therapy sessions, and spiritual disciplines. This "turning up the heat" reduces the soul of the practitioner to prime matter where it is transformed by contact with the primitive ground or birthplace of consciousness. Matter and spirit contend over the soul; soul is enriched through deep immersion in both.

The purified soul, infused by spirit, reconstitutes in a more perfect state, and, in fact, embodies the healing potential of the Philosopher's Stone. The person connected with this healing center gains the ability to heal others simply through contact with them. Their very presence is therapeutic, and others seek them out to bask in their energies. The embodiment of this force is the Wounded Healer. The previous radical psychic breakdown is finally resolved at a higher level of awareness.

Since psyche includes both body and soul, the addition of the missing spiritual element reunifies body, soul, and spirit in the alchemical *Unus Mundus*, the "one world," resulting in a holistic lifestyle and perspective. Ego realizes it is no longer the center of consciousness, even of the personality. Having touched the bottom of the abyss and survived its communion with primal Being, the soul can begin its ascent to the mountain top. The regenerative process is only begun, and integration becomes the goal.

Feminine right brain and masculine left brain processes are both honored, creating an inner marriage within the individual life. This royal wedding initiates an entirely new condition with its own potentialities. Ego develops a more rewarding life strategy, and soul finds fulfillment through the spiritual quest.

The self-destructive capacities of the individual are realized in the death-rebirth struggle. For some this manifests as an unconscious battle with addictive behaviors. If these self-destructive tendencies can be raised into consciousness, they are eventually diffused through increasing connection with the higher power. This is the process outlined by the multitude of recovery programs available for various addictions, ranging from abuse of alcohol and drugs, to food and sex, and other physical substitutes for meeting legitimate human needs in a mature, nontoxic manner.

Through various therapeutic processes, destructive energy is discharged consciously, and aggressive tendencies are reduced. Recovery becomes possible largely through rebirth in the spirit. Each therapeutic session moves the aspirant's philosophy toward a more mystical worldview, in line with his current experiences. As a by-product, experiential self-exploration leads to emotional and psychosomatic healing.

In the text, the two birds represent the conflict between spirit and the body. They fight and devour one another. One must slowly heat the material so that the body becomes white and the spirit red. The whitening operation is called *albedo*, and the reddening is *rubedo*. The birds remain bound together in a form of *coagulatio* or bondage that represents our confinement by actual reality to our portion of destiny. The Red and White represent a certain point in the alchemical process when the spirit and matter have almost become one. Spirit is becoming fixed in matter. This is almost the last practical step in the individuation process. The two complementarities are now almost synthesized in one entity.

The ego, heated by the reality of the conflict, allows the soul (the dove) to ascend as the sublimate. From this white dove is born a black, immortal Phoenix. The passion of the ego for adhering to its limited logic has finally completely burnt itself out. This allows the new answer of the self to arise, and arise it does in transpersonal form. This is the phoenix arising from the ashes. The ash comes from the *calcinatio* fire. It is the white ash of *albedo*, containing the opposites of despair, mourning, or repentance, and the Philosopher's Stone. It symbolizes the purity of the glorified body. The phoenix or spiritual body is born and brings with it many new emergent potentialities. Spirit and matter, having devoured one another, have reached a point of equilibrium.

Psychologically, spirit is now free to express itself through the personality level. On the other hand, personality finds the purpose of its creation in spiritual practice. There is a harmonization of the evolving personality with the incarnating Self. There is mutual interaction through the process of distillation between the heights and the depths, the light and the dark, the masculine and the feminine. You experience life even more consciously as both a psychological entity and as a soul. There is a further octave of development beyond this point, for which the enlightened personality is a vehicle. It is now possible to connect with your inner genius, your daemon. But even at this stage the personality is not perfected, for some geniuses are good and others are evil.

When the feminine is raised to a new level of awareness, even matter is not viewed as being dark and opaque, but rather as containing its own soft, vibrant inner light. This brings a reconciliation with your corporeal existence instead of a denial of body by a disembodied spiritual drive. Honoring the feminine also means an improvement in male/female relationships. Harmonization of masculine and feminine energies within yourself leads to their blending in the androgynous self. Mature men and women experience relationships through the bond of their common humanity, rather than as a bondage to outworn social forms. What is needed is discriminating integration of the unconscious feminine.

Jungian poet Robert Bly has captured the essence of this shifting awareness in a complement to the Lord's Prayer, a paean to the goddess, "A Mother's Prayer":

> Our Mother who are in earth, your name was always holy. Your kingdom has already arrived here in the body. May we sense what the whole universe wants to be, both in the body and in the spirit. May we make our own bread every day, and may we forgive everyone, even those who have not transgressed against us. Do not lead us into sickness, and save us from the longing we have to damage ourselves. For the body is yours, and delight, and ecstasy, forever and ever. Amen.

Matter and spirit continually pull the soul in opposite directions. The alienated soul is sucked down into the abyss of the primal unconscious until it reaches the bottom; yet it also feels the magnetic pull of its spiritual home. The alienated ego rejects both matter and spirit, body and mystical awareness. The body is cut off from the ego consciousness through a betrayal of trust. Frequently this happens in childhood through betrayal or abandonment by the parents. They may take good care of the physical needs of the child but fail to nourish the budding soul. The betrayal is making the child feel guilty for not living up to the parental notion of what that child should be. Betrayal of any kind creates fertile ground for the creation of addictive patterns. Healing comes when the ego learns to trust, despite the childhood betrayal of its essential being.

As the ego learns to trust the higher power, it also begins to trust and listen to its body, and self-destructive or self-defeating behaviors become more and more infrequent. Finding the core of the trauma, the original abandonment of soul, is very liberating. It frees you of the tyranny of the body, which has been exploited under the spell of the inner magician, a negative form of inner wisdom figure. Mesmerism by the dark magician leads to addiction and death; but connection with the lighter side of the archetype, the wise old man, moves the soul toward creativity.

Your soul may have initially been abandoned, but you do not have to continue in that mode by abandoning yourself. The trauma held in the body can be released in therapy sessions, with cleansing results for body, soul, and spirit. When the body is purified, the spirit can inhabit, or incarnate, in the body. The betrayal must be raised to consciousness. Increasing reliance is then placed on the higher power through faith, trust, and surrender. To surrender requires a receptive, feminine attitude, and a matrix for transformation strong enough to endure the unknown. Then, you may harmonize spirituality and instinct.

The alternative is to remain in an escapist trap, manically pursuing instant gratification through drugs, food, shopping, sex, alcohol, gambling. This soul-denying behavior is engaged in for a "high," but the compulsive style is regressive. Its bliss, ecstasy, and energy are unconscious, so no treasure is brought back for daily life. If you consciously take an active stand and disidentify from your devouring appetites for intoxication, sexuality, or food, you can learn to discipline your instincts. These powerful drives have been damaged through abuse, but you can channel those energies in more positive ways.

In contrast, the bliss of regeneration marks the end of ecstatic intoxications and the transition to a higher, joyous sobriety. It consists of transports, insights, glorious exaltations, contemplative absorptions, and feelings of blessedness. The spiritual inebriation gradually gives way to a serene joy in being. Taming of the instincts means relief for the ego from compelling urges and unmanageable cravings. All the stored repressed energy of the instincts has been defused, and they have lost their compulsive power. The instincts now aid in the actualization of your higher potential.

When you reinhabit your body at this stage you may experience undreamed-of physical delights and indulge your carnal appetites for a time. This may threaten your ego and its "head trips." But eventually ego comes to recognize the body as its holy temple, its immediate experience of the

Self. Ego admits its material nature, and reidentifies with the body. The ego is now anchored in each *chakra*, and connects with the soul, rooted in the seat of the body. This grounds the normally cerebral ego with a new earthiness and gut-reaction, a visceral wisdom.

Disruptions of mental functioning fade into the background due to an infusion of positive creative energy. Some of this energy takes the form of contemplation in a powerfully lucid, yet serene way. Ego is not blown away, but transported to a higher reality. Spontaneous inner images change from wrathful beings to benevolent inhabitants of celestial heights. Ego surrenders to an inflowing of spiritual energy; spirit incarnates in personalized form. If the inflowing energy is powerful, the person experiencing this stage may be intensely vital or charismatic.

Creative insight and spiritual dynamism can have a profound effect on others, but in this case the ego does not take credit since it is merely a channel for spirit. Phenomena associated with this include prophecy, spiritual healing, and other psychic anomalies. It feels like purgatory, because you have been raised up from hell and are so close to heaven. The sense of blessedness comes from the ego's realization that salvation is at hand.

Spirit is attracted to matter and vice versa. The right synthesis of "matter" or personality with the human spirit results in the expression of the spiritual man of earth. This is the true genius and the real means by which we may control conditions on our mental, emotional, and material levels. We may govern our environment through right attitude, and avoid being governed by it.

The white dove represents the *albedo* or purification process, which is the first goal of the Great Work. It is symbolic of the mental union of spirit and soul, uniting conceptually, sharing the same thoughts and direction. It occurs after the *nigredo* has divided the world into mind and matter, yet before the *rubedo* restores this spiritualized subtle body to its physical body. Alchemical warnings about the "reddening coming too fast" relate to the *rubedo* occurring before consciousness is prepared. The "whitening" is essential to slow this reddening. It also raises the blackness of the *nigredo* from its inertia.

Coagulatio is embodiment; *rubedo* enlivenment. *Albedo* is catharsis, a purifying of the emotions through the effect of art. *Albedo* is therefore an in-between state. It is a psychic reality that is both closely attached to what it joins and yet is distinct from it. Within the *albedo* phase you learn about the nature of psychic reality. During the *albedo* you come to understand how reality becomes psychic, and how psyche becomes real. Both have a strong imaginal component which corresponds with feminine symbols such as *anima,* luna, silver, the moon, dawn, and the white dove.

In the *albedo* phase, rather than being introverted or extroverted, you live in an "as if" reality where the differences between soul and external things no longer matters. Both inner and outer worlds are real. You no longer imagine things in the concrete, literal, material terms of the *nigredo.* And you are freed of the unconscious fascination of *participation mystique.* Even the sense of enchantment matures into a sense of hallowed resplendence. The magical world of enchantment is the middle ground between daily life and the earthly heaven of integration.

As the print shows, at this stage the ego is still in the woods, and enchanted woods at that. Its salvation is allowing metaphor and symbol to bridge the gap between matter and spirit. Through metaphor one object is likened to another by speaking of it "as if" it were that other. It has been called the imaging of spirit in matter, or even spirit as matter. The world of soul lies between matter and spirit and is the realm where metaphor provides the means of communication. Here, imagination *is* reality. It is the realm of the subtle body, that body through which we express our essential beingness.

The soul joins heaven and earth through metaphor by integrating images with feeling, mind, and imagination. The healing power of both metaphor and symbol comes from its impact on the total person. Metaphor nourishes the imagination and heart, as well as the mind. When you consciously employ right-brain thinking to enrich your experience, your process may lead you to dancing, singing, painting, writing, and other creative modalities. Metaphor allows the process to flow and transform, unlocking habitual patterns. In the imaginal world, your process presents you with healing symbols that allow the split between spirit and matter to heal. In a metaphorical reality you can suspend disbelief in the spirit of play and surrender to the process.

You can develop a more feminine perspective on life to balance your rational attitudes. This has been termed lunar- or *anima*-consciousness in Jungian psychology. It offers an alternative to the limitations of ego's viewpoint. Seeing, listening, and attending all shift from the gross attachments of the *nigredo* to a new transparence and resonance. Truly the world seems miraculous and sublime for you can now perceive the animating power of the primal force within everything. You see soul in all natural objects. The world seems lustrous, scintillating with a brilliant radiance and sheen. Things begin to shine and speak; they are "animated" and suffused with soul.

Symbols can be classed according to the archetype they embody. Through the underlying essence of the archetype, certain symbols share common qualities. For example, symbols standing for the Sun include gold, diamond, yellow, the lion with its fiery mane, and so forth. Symbols found in a unique context, such as in dreams, create images. These images are subtle bodies which communicate a message through the soul by showing their special essential qualities. In this correspondence system, like attracts like. Entities and objects that have a common archetypal core are imaginally grouped together. For example, the correspondence list for *albedo* could be continued past moon, silver, and dove, to the goddess Artemis or Diana; her sacred animal is the dog; her stones moonstone, pearl, or crystal; the plants include hazel and moonwort; the scents camphor and aloes, etc.

This whitening phase refers to the emergence of a psychological consciousness. You have the ability to perceive fantasy creating reality. In this phase all occurrences begin as images; they must first be imagined. The alchemical white becomes present in any object or body once you seek it as an image, through metaphor or analogy. Simply ask yourself this simple series of questions to develop a metaphor from a vague feeling:

(1) What would you like to have happen?

(2) When it's not happening, how do you know, and where do you feel it in your body?

(3) It is more on the inside or the outside?

(4) What's it like?

(5) Does it have a shape? What size is it? Does it have color, temperature, or movement?

(6) What could it be made of?

Take some time to know about that metaphor, and all the qualities of that metaphor, and what that metaphor is doing. Become that image, sensing its essence. What would that metaphor like to have happen, and what would that metaphor like to do?

Whitening gives the *anima* and your feminine awareness direct experience of its innate power. This power comes from the blackness or shadow. It has not been washed away; rather, it is built into the psyche's body and has become transparent enough to see through. Spirit is restored to matter. Will and compulsion are now seen as more than just desire. They express transformative passion. As alchemists, we see them as soul. The mind may be inflamed by the hot urge to action and lose its reflective ability. It may be cooled by a weepy deluge, inspired by an *anima* mood. It is difficult to turn inward and see through to the meaning for your soul when you must compulsively "act out" every urge or desire. When liberated of the compulsion to act out, the gratitude of blessed release cools down the ecstatic happiness into a feeling of being favored by the divine forces.

Resistance to change is difficult to overcome, even when the rewards are the fruits of the tree of life. Only intense heat can move human nature from its inborn inertia and love of the status quo. You may have to turn up the heat (*rubedo*) to prevent cooling and separate the body from soul. The Phoenix, however, is rejuvenated by immersion in fire. The alchemist may have to invite new passions and aggressions, forcing confrontations on vital questions that the white lady (*anima*) might prefer to cool. Therapeutic support means feeding the fire.

This fire can be seen as your Guardian Angel and spirit, for aspiration guards the angel from cooling. In other words, you need to create a time and place in your life to honor your process by combining passive fantasy with active imagination. When you enter actively into right-brain experience you undergo a profound transformation of consciousness, which is healing and regenerates your spiritual life. Direct experience of the psychic reality of imaginal life is very enriching.

Active imagination allows you to grapple with the angel of your unique destiny. These angels, mediating between heaven and earth, constitute the ascents and descents of the soul. Alchemy is a metaphor for the transformation process. It is a form of code that directly appeals to the unconscious. It includes a system of mind-training through which spiritual qualities can be accessed by the controlled use of imagination.

The text alludes to a "Forest in India." India is the body as holy temple. The forest is the neural network within the aspirant's body. The white and red birds in this context are still bound together. We can imagine them as the interlacing channels of *ida* and *pingala* from Eastern philosophy. White is *ida*; red is *pingala*. They are channels for energy circulation in the subtle body of the yogi.

When they balance, the middle channel or *sushumna* opens, allowing the *kundalini* to rise. This produces mystical ecstasy. Again, the idea is a balance or marriage of opposites. The Western symbol of this system is the Caduceus, representing the two poles of the psyche united in an integrated duality through the spirit. Whether religion, psychology, alchemy, or yoga is the metaphor of choice, the process is the same.

The Jewish symbol of divine balance and union is the Star of David. It consists of an upward pointing equilateral triangle which symbolizes fire or spirit (△), and a downward pointing triangle which symbolizes water or matter (▽). Interlocked they form a grand symbol of integration, the six-pointed star of wholeness (✿). The equal-armed cross symbolizes the union of the four elements. The Christian Cross shows that the agony of experiencing opposites simultaneously is equated with crucifixion.

This first section of Lambsprinck's process has shown a metamorphosis of soul. The first eight plates show the heights and depths of human character. They refer to a simple cycle of transformation, or system for resolving inner conflicts and moving toward integration of the personality. In summary, the plates show the following:

Plate 1: Primordial unity of instinctual consciousness; harmonious unification; *fusion*. Ego is enveloped, immersed, enmeshed.

Plate 2: Opposites emerge in an image of *conflict*.

Plate 3: The struggle creates imbalance in the psyche activating the law of *compensation*.

Plate 4: This depicts the pendulum swing to the opposite attitude, *oscillation*.

Plate 5: Represents the danger of *fixating* on one of the opposites to solve the conflict.

Plate 6: A balanced tension of opposites promotes the *circulation* of energy and stiumulates transformation.

Plate 7: Dynamic *interchange* and regulation creates a new unity which resolves the original conflict.

Plate 8: The new harmonious *unification* contains opposites that are discrete yet conjoined through a reconciling factor, the transpersonal Self.

Through therapy or personal growth you learn how to open up to your own inner process. The second octave of the Lambsprinck process concerns personal experience of the transcendent dimension. Through direct mystical experience of the divine you learn how to carry on with that process. It means the realization of the transpersonal Self is an essentially religious endeavor. Therapy is the process of unifying the conflicting drives within an individual. It is like a "tune up" for a more spiritual life. Once a person experiences a high degree of integration a whole new world opens, truly a "new life," tending toward joy and perfection.

Embracing the opposites and integrating their powerful energies is a supreme human achievement. They include not only the polarities of sensuality and spirituality, female and male, but also inner and outer, nature and science, the one and the many, chaos and order, creativity and business, and individual and planet (or environment). It is a biocentric, not egocentric consciousness. By engaging these energies you can discover their transpersonal potential for your liberation and that of the human race. The Philosopher's Stone is produced by the union of purified opposites, those with which the ego no longer identifies.

In alchemy, the marriage of opposites is called *coniunctio*. The *coniunctio* is a new perspective or standpoint that allows you to experience the opposites simultaneously. It produces both a new freedom and a new burden of knowledge that good and evil, for example, persist throughout psychic life. The Stone symbolizes the love of wisdom made practical or concrete. It is a metaphor for the solid grounding of spirituality in practical life. The outer aspect of *coniunctio* motivates us to connect in social systems, the inner aspect to connect with the Self.

The net result is an individual who is not only functional, but able to perform at higher levels of effectiveness. The difference between dysfunctionality, functionality, and performance is great. For example, any old car can function as transportation, but it barely resembles a high-performance vehicle. The marriage or coincidence of opposites is a state where you feel the plenitude of all opposites in fusion without conflict. Nostalgia for the primal unity and the sense of fragmentation are healed in a higher synthesis. Some approach this state to a greater or lesser degree.

The dichotomy of love and will is another way to experience the opposites. Another expression is practicality versus idealism or mysticism. We have spoken of the psychological polarity between mind and feeling, but this is just a sub-theme of the cosmic polarity of Eros and Logos. Eros is the driving power of libido, psychic energy. Logos is the principle of order, law, harmony, beauty, and discipline. Discipline also contrasts with spontaneity. There are many other aspects of psychological life to be harmonized in different ways including intuition and logic, prudence and adventurousness, optimism and pessimism, and conservatism and renewal. Our oscillations between the poles may last a few moments or stretch into years.

The solution offered in psychosynthesis is to remain conscious of both poles, identifying with neither, and moving toward a creative tension. By identifying with the Self, which encompasses and supercedes both, you gain independence. From the vantage-point of the Self, you can regulate their interplay in your life through rhythmical expression. For example, you have probably noticed the rhythmic interplay between your introversion and extroversion, work and play, contemplation and action. The perception of contrast lessens in convergence or synthesis. For instance, when you "follow your bliss," to pursue your vocation or work seems fun like play.

When the opposites balance one another, a higher degree of integration is possible. You are free to be both loving and strong, practical and idealistic, crazy and logical, dreamy and organized. The interplay of qualities and resources are available at appropriate times and on call by the conscious personality. The grand *coniunctio* is the operation of the sun, and leads to the first stage of the continuing transpersonal process, *solificatio*. This commences the second half of Lambsprinck's process.

PART II

Spiritual Development

PART II

Spiritual Development

A human being is a part of a whole, called by us "universe." A part limited in time and space. He experiences himself, his thoughts and feelings as something separated from the rest—a kind of optical delusion of his consciousness. This delusion is a kind of prison for us, restricting us to our personal desires, and to affection for a few persons nearest us. Our task must be to free ourselves from this prison by widening our circle of compassion to embrace all living creatures and the whole nature in its beauty. Nobody is able to achieve this completely, but the striving for such achievement is, in itself, a part of the liberation, and a foundation for inner security.

—Albert Einstein

THE experience of spiritual awakening represents a quantum leap in consciousness. Part I of Lambsprinck's process alludes to a "tuning up" of the personality, making it more effective in the world. Psychologically, it is an exploration of the depths leading to increased self-acceptance. Now the seeker gains access to the heights.

Prior to spiritual awakening, you spent a lot of your existence "holding back." At first it seemed like holding back the pain of your own personal traumas and tragedies. Then the focus shifted to the emerging subconscious whose downward pull definitely provokes defensiveness. From this point on, you are strenuously holding back your enlightenment. Every itch and ache during meditation helps to protect your ego. When both of these levels are processing or clearing, awareness of an emerging spiritual reality begins to build within you. Seeking release, you begin on the spiritual path.

Your life is a process of self-realization. Your consciousness is rising to a new level. You are maturing away from rationalization, fear, resistance, escape, commitment-phobia, ego-death paranoia, profaning the sacred. Your movement is toward creativity, joy, contentment, transcendence, insight, harmony, beauty, compassion, bliss, and Higher Power.

This is the realm of the subtle or causal body, sometimes referred to as the *Body of Light*. For mystics the goal is union with the Higher Power and meditation is the method of choice. Through meditation, you climb to the summit of your own consciousness, and there you find God. The spiritual mandate of human evolution is unity. This evolutionary process initiates transformation through symbols and imagery.

This evokes a responsive series of refinements which move consciousness to ever-higher levels. You find that your awareness transcends your personal self and enters the realm of the transpersonal. Your values widen into the ethical, aesthetic, heroic, humanitarian, altruistic, and creative. You learn to live your mythology consciously. You are becoming transparent to transcendence and experience what it means to suspend time, space, and your personal identity.

Through following your spiritual path, you come to awareness of the Whole and the holy nature of reality. Joseph Campbell called it learning to see yourself "depersonalized in the mirror of the human spirit." By practicing seeing through the eyes of the collective human spirit, you develop a radically different perspective on life. This eye of the human spirit, the *third eye* of the mystic East, is the transpersonal Self. The seeker of the awakening becomes the seer.

The seer views the transcendent Self and is seen by it. Over time the seer identifies with the Self, and I-Thou polarity dissolves. From the holistic perspective you embrace higher values, realize your inherent divinity, and enlarge your potentials. The boundary between the seer and the seen collapses into cosmic consciousness. The seer becomes a sage.

"The Lord of the Forest takes his Kingdom's Throne"

PLATE 9

Now hear a wonderful story,
What a great thing I report to you,
That the King Almighty pleads for you;

Hear what the High Noble says:
My enemy have I always fought,
I have trod the Dragon underfoot.

114

I am a Lord and King in the Earth.
None may be born over me,
Neither by Art or Nature,
Or any living creature.

I achieve all that man can desire,
I can provide you what you need,
Giving power and health with more abundant life;
Also gold, silver, pearls and precious stones,
Together with all kinds of medicine.

For first I was of low birth,
But I was raised,
And advanced on high.

God and Nature have granted it,
So that from the worst I became the best,
Arriving at the great throne
To assume kingly rank.
Therefore Hermes calls me Lord of the Forests.

The Lord of the Forests takes his Kingdom's throne,
Now grown from lowest to highest degree.

If fortune smiles, you will become Consul from Rhetor.
If fortune frowns, you will become Rhetor from Consul.

Understand truly that you have seen the first step in
the preparation of the Tincture.

"The Lord of the Forest takes his Kingdom's Throne."

Chapter 9: Hero

Solificatio

THE crowned king shows the human spirit ruling in man when personality is exalted with wisdom and achievement. In humanistic terms, this king who sits on his throne surrounded by symbols of his power represents self-actualization. In his right hand he holds the orb of the world, with the cross of the four elements above it in equilibrium. This phase constellates an identification of personality with the archetype of the positive hero.

Symbolically the king represents universal or archetypal man. He usually is described in myth as having magical power or other supernatural resources at his command. He embodies the ruling or governing principle, supreme consciousness, and the virtues of sound judgement and self-control. The kingly figure shares some aspects in common with the positive expression of the Freudian superego.

We each embody the king in times of achievement, personal victory, or moments of consummation (*coniunctio*). In Greece, both bridegroom and bride wear a crown to symbolize their exalted state. When you reach the stage of life where your potential is manifesting and your dreams are being realized, you are indeed kingly. You wear the crowning glory of success, not just the conformist mask of consumerism. You are also the hero. You are able to actualize your will for the greater good. Your subjective and objective realities are in harmony. The king is like the Superior Man of the *I Ching*, who is in tune with the Tao. There is a resolution of the personal turmoil of the first stage when the personality had to make so many adjustments and compromises.

The king is adept at creating his own reality and does so with intent. In his left hand he holds the scepter of power. The Dragon, symbol of the instinctual world of the *anima mundi* and the raw forces of the elements, lies at his feet. His throne is supported by the dolphin of inspiration. The seven steps leading up to the throne symbolize the seven planes or changes in consciousness required to reach this phase. Crowning is the emergence of the spiritual principle of Light into conscious life.

In alchemy the figure of the king—King Sol—indicates a special form of consciousness. It is experience of one's own inner essence, or Self, as a being of Light. This king symbolizes the dominant force in the psyche, which

117

determines your values. Identification with its power and virtues are experienced as renewal for the rational consciousness.

In terms of human consciousness, this king brings the alchemist nearer to the qualities represented by the Sun—clarity, creativity, lucidity, moderation, courage, tact, and the wisdom born of self-knowledge. The king represents the inner truth, the integrity that brings the healing of our inner conflicts. *Solificatio*, as an operation, is the sublimation of desire into aspiration, moving from the lower to the higher mind. The potentials of the individual's entire mind-body system are activated and available.

Interaction of conscious will with that of the Self creates the possibility of actually fulfilling your unique potential. There is a subtle shift in identity, from shifting identification to the totality of the I Am Self. This brings with it a new responsibility for your ways of *being-in-the-world*. Choices become more conscious and intentional. It is not even the will of an ego in service to the superego, but a spontaneous decision of the whole mind-body being.

The self-conscious individual simultaneously experiences the world through sensations, perceptions, biological urges, emotions, beliefs, thoughts, and self-reflection. This self-aware personality has mastered the primary aspects of life as symbolized by the lower six *chakras*. These include survival, sexuality, power, love, communication, and self-reflection. The work of the crown *chakra*, developing further potential for wisdom and self-realization leads to the potential for cosmic consciousness, a deep sense of integration with the universe.

Part I of Lambsprinck is concerned with the metamorphosis of an individual's feminine aspect. This process is repeated in the consciousness of every alchemist and seeker after psychological transformation. *Solificatio*, on the other hand, deals with the conscious differentiation of the masculine aspect of existence. *Solificatio* is a symbol of the source of life and the ultimate wholeness of man. It is the illumination which takes place inside the head. We refer to this state as "enlightenment." A halo or aura around the head often symbolizes this spiritual illumination in art or legend. The enlightened King Sol introduces the human element into the Lambsprinck symbolism and represents a renewal of consciousness which harmonizes body and spirit simultaneously.

The philosopher-king of the *solificatio* phase is an archetypal character. In later plates, different aspects of the king are represented by father, son, and spiritual guide. These represent physical, spiritual, and soul aspects, respectively. No one human being can ever realize all of his potentials, symbolized by the son. Even an alchemist who is able to experience individual wholeness cannot appropriate the entire range of mankind's heights and depths into his repertoire.

Solificatio does provide a major increase in philosophical insight. This insight, in turn, leads to the formulation of unique "*sol*-utions" in various aspects of life. Jung pointed out that "the doubts of the philosopher are dissolved through his insight." This insight is made possible by the clear radiance of the Spirit shining within. This inner light has been linked with solar symbolism and the Self, as in the writings of the Islamic mystic Hallaj:

> The Sun of the One I love has risen in the night,
> Resplendent, and there will be no more sunset . . .
> I saw my Lord with the eye of the heart, and I said
> "Who are you?" and he said "Your Self."

But no one individual can successfully embody the archetype of the Self. None of us could claim all of the nobility and beauty of mankind's potential as a species. Since the archetype of the Self is bipolar, good and bad, it would also mean an inhuman acceptance of all the guilt for the evils manifesting in daily life around the world.

We connect with Self most deeply by dealing with our portion of destiny, acknowledging the meaning and mystery that underlie our objective reality. Consciousness is able to expand the scope of our perceptions through self-development, but only within our specific, unique limitations.

This plate symbolizes the ruling principle of total being. When the ego gives up its central position in the psyche to the Self, it experiences a sense of immortality. The ego is reborn as the Self, symbolized by the "king of the world." This is the symbolism of the archetypal pattern of the hero-savior. The hero archetype, while linked with the mythic themes of divine child and Great Mother, tends to merge at maturity with the figure of the King and the Wise Old Man. His destiny is the dangerous adventure, the magical quest, or the impossible deed. The philosopher-king pursues the mystical quest.

Examples of projecting the hero archetype outside of oneself are many. These are our culture heroes, like favorite athletes, entertainers, politicians, or spiritual leaders. This archetype can also invade a personality, compulsively driving a person to act out the role of this king literally. However, he would never achieve a sense of wholeness, since identifying with the Great Light means denying or rejecting the shadow side of human life. This has been the downfall of many successful religious leaders, revealing a pathological imbalance.

Women experience this archetype through the positive *animus* as wayshower in life. When we set out to learn about ourselves, we plan a great journey into the depths of our psyche, echoing great literary themes and legends like those of Siddhartha and King Arthur. The hero does not overcome evil. Rather, he wins the ability to overcome his infantile self and realize that good and bad are aspects of the total nature of being. This allows a breakthrough past personal limitations leading toward spiritual growth.

The illustration indicates that the *Lord of the Forests* has risen from the bestial depths to the highest position in cultural values. With his personality harmonized, he is a successful king of the material level of existence. This indicates that the Tincture has reached its first degree of perfection— the king holds dominion over the land. The implication is that the law of moderation and the axiom of Self-knowledge hold sway.

Jung has indicted that the deepening and broadening of consciousness through the raising of unconscious contents from the depths is a spiritual act which constitutes an "enlightenment." What was formerly hidden in darkness comes up to be revealed in the light of conscious awareness. He elaborates further on the relationship of the king symbol to consciousness by intimating that when the symbolism of the mighty king appears it is the new dominant of consciousness, which is no longer under the dominion of the unconscious and hidden in darkness. King, sun, or lion all refer to the power instinct of the ego and are subject to further transformation in the alchemical process.

Coniunctio is the operation of the sun. During the process of *coniunctio* there is an ego death for the old style of consciousness; renewal does not occur until instinctual desire has been transmuted into spirit or conscious understanding. This emergent consciousness has gained the ability to experience opposites at the same time, including good and evil.

The kingly individual is also characterized by expressions of transpersonal love. The balance of the personality comes from an introverted connection with the Self working with an extroverted social conscience. One direction leads to unity with the Self, the other to unity with mankind. In either case, the activated Self provides the motivational energy, whether meditating on the inside or mobilizing outwardly. The ability of the superior person to inspire others into active commitment comes from the contagious effect emanated from the Self in action.

The alchemical concept of God as *senex* (Father) and *puer* (Son) is a variation on the theme of the king's renewal. This metaphor appears in both philosophy and ecclesiastical circles. Jung alludes to it, stating that

King Sol represents renewed consciousness.

This renewal leads to a powerful transformation of lifestyle that may lead to an identification with the hero archetype or the "mana personality." The hero's pattern of quest, deliverance, discovery, and great deeds echoes the main themes of the process of psychological transformation. When we set out to learn about ourselves, we plan a great journey into the depths of our psyche. The richness found within this experience is reflected in great literature and art.

If you pursue self-knowledge in the depths of the psyche, you need to learn how to swim in that oceanic environment. Otherwise, you may wind up drowning in emotional chaos, swallowed up like Jonah by the whale. Therefore, at a certain level in your quest for the Grail, it is appropriate to have strong "coping" and "heroic" ego attitudes. These help your ego remain oriented toward the Light as its goal and provide it with resolve and courage required to penetrate further depths, which are currently hidden from your view.

Joseph Campbell has popularized the hero archetype and its characteristic traits. These include a sometimes miraculous or peculiar birth; sometimes abandonment (innocent/orphan); a period of seemingly aimless wandering (wanderer); overcoming obstacles sometimes by divine intervention (martyr); gaining the treasure which is hard to find and difficult to hold onto (warrior); and a returning home or reunion (shaman/magician).

As an archetype, the paradoxical nature of the hero may be positive or negative, progressive or regressive. The text alludes to this karmic fortune in the references to consul and rhetor. A rhetor is an orator or teacher while a consul is a chief magistrate. The text indicates that if fortune smiles, you are promoted; if it frowns there is demotion, or regression back to a lower condition. The hero can move in a regressive submission to the mother (or unconscious), which repeats the incestuous tendency of Oedipus.

Alternatively, the masculine energies within us can expand our consciousness both regressively and progressively, uniting our history with our futurity. We do this by living out our unique portion of destiny. This leads to the conscious mind's ability to experience the unity of the psyche. And this process is linked to self-realization.

This quest is inherently dangerous, especially in the early stages. Hence, the sense of adventure. The crises and danger have the potential of destroying the personality. When the hero descends into the underworld (unconscious), he must discard the defenses of conscious development (for example, intellect). But he gains a mythical type of awareness that allows him to experience directly the paradoxical aspect of the archetypes without going insane. The ego filters the archetypal power and protects the personality. The archetype functions as a sender, ego as receiver. The archetype plays through you, but ego does not identify with it.

As the hero, you come to understand that you contain both of your parental images as well as the archetypal parental images that made your parents seem like gods when you were small. Comprehending this leads to an understanding of your essentially androgynous nature. You realize experientially that you are composed of both masculine and feminine aspects. The symbol of this androgyny is an image of wholeness. It is a way of uniting opposites within yourself rather than seeking to overcome them through conflict and confrontation. The uniting symbol resolves the tension of opposites.

The goal of the hero's quest is a higher synthesis of the ego, with access to both the conscious and the unconscious. Your maturing through the hero means you learn to transform your conflicts into a nobler and more stable personality with deep roots in the sources of life. As hero, you are involved in a paradoxical process of ordering, which is precisely why you may be susceptible to breakdown or wounding. You are assaulted by the forces of chaos, entropy, and disorder, as well as the forces of negative entropy. It is a paradoxical truth that acts of ordering can result in potential weakening of the ego. As hero, you learn to withstand the effects of the disorder that your creative efforts prompt.

When the king alludes to having "trod the dragon underfoot" it reveals an ego attitude perhaps healthier in the medieval mind than in today's world. Many Jungians feel that the myth of the heroic dragon-slaying sun hero has moved on to overkill. Yes, we must struggle to win our consciousness from the regressive pull of the Great Mother's world. But this transformative urge taken to excess has resulted in technological rape of the planet nearly killing Mother Earth. And still we are not really free of the Mother, but worship her in concrete materialism, consumerism, compulsive behavior, and spiritual materialism.

Dragon-slaying must be understood as a symbolic process of transformation; then the feminine is not torn asunder from matter. As Marion Woodman writes,

> Consciously relating to the Great Mother is coming back to the garden and recognizing the place for the first time, recognizing that it is a garden and that we have dishonored it. Consciousness takes an ego stand and refuses to identify with devouring appetites for food, drink, sexuality. It refuses to fall into compulsive behavior. By disciplining

the power drives of instincts that are damaged because they have been abused, consciousness opens the way for love, rather than the compulsion of the dragon-slaying vow to kill the mother in order to be free of her dark womb.

As we learn to honor the feminine and find balance within our personalities, we stop repressing it and allow it full emergence into consciousness. This is one way of nurturing the growth of your own soul and your creativity. It is the process of soul-making, for the soul is conscious femininity. It is also the embodiment of Spirit, the receiver of Spirit. Soul becomes conscious through the agency of metaphor as the symbol flows between spirit and matter healing the split.

Another drawback of the heroic ego is that its time sense is strictly linear. That was fine for consciousness when Newtonian physics prevailed; in the quantum age it is obsolete. If you identify too strongly with this inner figure, you can never arrive in some future time at the transcendent reality *now*. You can never experience unity in consciousness as you obsessively move *toward* it. The trick is to relate to archetypes rather than identify with them.

Your goal, as hero, in psychological terms, is to train your ego to function at the threshold of the conscious and subconscious worlds effectively. You may learn to extract guidance and meaning from the unconscious without having to sink into a trance state or an imaginal state. In other words, you receive direct guidance, rather than having to interpret vague impressions or symbolism. Psychology leads us toward this ability. The path of individuation means we learn to see psychological patterns at work in our life, without going into a trance to do so. Other emergent powers become stabilized also.

As hero, your first feat is to clarify your psychological difficulties, clear the blocks, voyage to the edge of your own known world, and win the treasure of direct experience and assimilation of the archetypal images. You'll have to battle your personal historical limitations to obtain the vision of the well-springs of human existence. Then your second task, of returning to normal life as a transformed teacher of the way within, must begin. In the initial stage, you assimilate; later you disseminate.

If the would-be hero doesn't submit to all the initiatory tests and steals the treasure, the powers of the unconscious are mobilized to blast him from within and without. This is imagined as crucifixion or eternal torment. And how many of us have our crosses to bear! One face of the hero is the martyr who must learn how to give up. But if we learn the virtues of the path and practice them, a self-centered ego can become centered in transpersonal reality, and we may emerge as a cultural hero or heroine.

Your inner hero-self may at first refuse the call to adventure. In the stories, some supernatural entity intervenes and the quest is on. You're off to see the wizard. The rough, unfamiliar terrain, the crossroads, and the gauntlet of initiatory barriers mirror the ordeals of the inner quest. But adversity may be followed by many preliminary victories in the form of unretainable ecstasies. You realize you cannot ultimately conquer evil. But you can overcome your infantile sentimentalities and resentments and realize that good and bad are contained in the masculine law and feminine image of the nature of being.

The agony of breaking through your personal limitations is the very process that leads to spiritual growth. To complete your task, however, you must return to your mundane life and try to integrate your inner experience. Identified with the hero, you are warrior, lover, ruler, and tyrant. When you return, you are truly human, no longer merely ego-oriented.

The hero within teaches culturally valued aspirations. It helps us move from a state of innocence and helplessness, through conformity, to a place of courage, faith, and joy. When the ego gains strength through attending to process in therapy, it feels less dependent, even enlightened or liberated. The personal ego concedes that it is not sufficient to guide personal life in any holistic way. At this stage you may realize a profound need for a spiritual authority that transcends ego. The search for one's Higher Power is begun in earnest.

We seek a path of spiritual or religious devotion and growth in order to continue the deepening process begun in therapy. This authority must spring from our deep historical or psychological roots. Once again, there is realization that the arrival of the new king means the ego must step into the background as the ruling principle of conscious life. The old king is dead; long live the king!

In order to seek actively in the divine dimension you must turn to some form of creative mysticism. In the course of individuation, this might be termed "process theology." There are at least two forms of spiritual growth. The first comes from your individual needs and responses to divinity, and constitutes religious development. The second, spiritual development, comes from examining the effect of grace on your life and functioning.

Meditation with a religious or spiritual goal marks the upper limit of mankind's mental efforts—it is a silent plea for grace. Through personal experience of your Higher Power, without the mediation of a priesthood, you formulate your own individual values and belief system. Your spirituality bears on your expression of integrity, how you conduct yourself in all areas of existence.

Your conscious ego can function as an integral part of your soul when it awakens to its task of meditation and becomes receptive. Then it may make contact with divine forces of sufficient purity to become a channel for the spirit. This channel is formed by intentionally turning your attention to the perception of the archetype of divinity. These archetypes are most commonly experienced as your image of God (religion), the Self (psychology), the Guardian Angel (alchemy), or the Guru (yoga and mysticism).

At this stage of aspiration you do not *become* divinity, but actively begin seeking unity with it. After all, most of our human activities and attachments actively keep our enlightenment at bay! Nonetheless, your mind can learn to tap channels of spiritual energy at will to transform either yourself or your environment. This is accomplished with a correct understanding of the nature of existence and its relationship to the human mind. Your mind is a powerful creative tool when attention and visualization are applied under the direction of spiritual guidance.

This ability of the mind to influence reality at this level makes high ethical standards a mandatory requirement. If we think we have deep insight into others' problems, we must realize that our interventions have the possibility of doing more harm than good. Therefore, if we choose to interact in the lives of others, we must realize that role may be catalytic, and any intervention must be noninvasive. One way of developing ethical standards is to relate to firm role models, spiritual teachers whose integrity we respect.

In terms of therapy, the king is associated with the symbolism of death and rebirth. The old king (the ego) had to die before the new king appeared in consciousness. Another arc of this pattern is repeated in the process of meditation. We enact the process of death/rebirth every day we practice meditation by withdrawal of the attention from sensory perception in the outside world. Mystics die daily. Through this method the mind is assigned its proper place in consciousness, which is a field encompassing the totality of reality. Through meditation, the ego yields "control" to the higher spiritual awareness, and the possibility of embodying the power of the true Self emerges.

Your intellect can participate in the life of the Spirit, but is not identical with it. For the sake of spiritual growth, you must train your mind to adhere to spiritual principles and disciplines despite your personal pain-pleasure cycle. In other words, once you embark upon knocking at the door for God, it behooves you to remain consistent in your daily meditation. Consistency of effort helps develop the integration of the personality with the higher Self. This manifests, for example, in Christians who would claim "It is not I, but Christ who lives in me."

This phase of illuminative development brings creativity in its wake, and verbal creativity in particular. Recall, the Rhetor of the text is a teacher of persuasive speech. This is the seed of charisma, which flowers in the *mana personality*, a topic discussed in the next chapter. A person at this stage not only understands their personal psychology pretty well, but can also discuss the condition of their soul. At this phase, your self reflection and awareness of behavior patterns leads to insight and the ability to share your story of personal growth.

Having named your demons (mother complex, *puer* complex, negative *senex*, etc.), you win a certain level of conscious realization in the external world (works, good acts) or in the internal (mystical meditation). Freed from the stress of over-reacting or under-reacting in the emotional sphere, you can flower through various modes of self-expression. A fluid relationship between your ego and subconscious is stabilizing.

The beginnings of the creative process lie in introspection on information previously assimilated. This may take many forms, such as focusing on a problem and studying all angles of it, with various options and consequences. After preparation and incubation, an illumination or answer to the problem may suddenly occur. Creativity is part of philosophy, for the creative spirit raises problems or questions, which we then seek to resolve through conceptual and verbal activity.

On the spiritual level, after you pass through the first phase of moral integration (the purgation period), you break through into the second stage of the spiritual life. This is the *illuminative way*, the path toward enlightenment. It is the middle phase of the spiritual journey which is the subjective experience of light, resulting from God's grace. The ecstasy of being penetrated or flooded by the light is a spontaneous mystical experience. Its potential unfolds when we can overcome our psychological barriers through therapy and drop our powerful defenses, thus becoming aware of God's presence within ourselves.

This illumination is preparation for union with God. It becomes easier to sustain loving devotion, to pray, to discard obstacles on the path, and offer humble service. If you fall down on your spiritual path, do not bother bemoaning the fact. Rather, pick yourself up and try again. As you relinquish your defensive denial and rationalizations, you must cope with some unruly aspects of the unconscious never-before encountered. Appropriate modes of aspiration for this phase include illuminative prayer and contemplative meditation. This illuminative path is not the final goal. Here you are still subject to vices, particularly spiritual pride.

Your self-image, which may have been traumatized during spiritual awakening and seeking, now has the chance for deep healing which comes from within, bringing increased inner strength. Since some maturity is required, this path usually opens up after midlife and focuses around the paradox of opposites. Practically, this means you are confronted with such issues as assertiveness, aggression, self-indulgence, self-gratification, and questions of dependence and independence.

The healthy choice is for an interdependence, as is shown in many recovery systems. This holds true within the psyche as well. The vivifying qualities of the archetypes are experienced in feelings of rejuvenation, quickening, healing, and nurturing.

There is an inherent risk in the illuminative way that has nothing to do with our previous mistakes, but is possible following any discipline. As you expose more of your real being, you activate and act out the powerful heights and depths of your potential for good or evil. Scrupulous honesty and integrity are the only safeguards that preserve you from spiritual suicide. Use faith, hope, and love as guides when you look into your own soul. Any self-hatred can be transformed into compassion, and compassion for oneself ultimately spreads outward.

Your shadow may have its beasts and demons, but the dark side of the hidden mind can reveal itself as "That which no one should have to face within." Having seen the darkness within, the challenge is to continue with faith and courage. Simply remember that as the light shines on your vices and pseudo-virtues, you need only to continue the process of refinement. However, the ante keeps rising: the more conscious you become, the more conscious you must be.

As your inner light increases, you may seem worse to yourself than you had thought. Shining a bright light in a corner reveals all the dirt. Your shortcomings were there all along, but now the light has exposed them. There is no need for cynicism or losing heart; simply continue with your meditation.

A spiritual director is the best way to avoid the dangers of any stage. Other hazards of this phase include zealous self-righteousness, spiritual greed, or a conviction that one is the special elect of God with a mission. Spiritual greed means not giving enough of ourselves to our responsibilities in outer life. If we "render unto Caesar," there is room in life for fulfilling both our outer duties and our inner spiritual practice.

The serious aspirant will seek to avoid pride, sensuality, and spiritual avarice throughout the day, and particularly at the time of meditation. Another pitfall is spiritual sloth or lukewarmness toward the path. A final trap is interfering inadvertently with someone else's spiritual growth, their true will. If your "mission from God" seems to be doing this, perhaps you should reexamine your calling.

The more creative you become, the easier it is to replace a lost project with a new one. Your intuition gives you access through the threshold of the unconscious to incredible creative powers which are the driving force behind genius, madman, and saint. The mystics realize this creative resource as a genius for transcendence. They come into their inspirational experience much like artists and poets. The emergence of this powerful energy appears as mystery. Some mystical experiences are spontaneous and unstructured, whiles others are structured and available on demand.

The emergent abilities now come when called for. They combine a spontaneous, revolutionary principle (*puer*) with the conservative influence (*senex*) of accumulation, knowledge, or technique. In mysticism, new insights occur more frequently when the mystic's intensive perception is unstructured, as in the nature mystic's intense experiences of light, peace, or unification. Unstructured experiences may be induced by an intense sexual experience, the awesomeness of nature, or some other external sensate means that temporarily enlarges or dissolves the boundaries of personal identity.

The I-Thou separation is beginning to lose meaning and moves toward unification in the realization that "I Am." Many people experience intense mystical feelings in nature which are deeply emotional and transformative. Mystics move from the lesser experience of strong emotion to a higher experience that transcends affect and ideation. The means is through some process of "trained transcendence." They practice a system which fosters spontaneous breakthrough of bliss, peace, serenity, even rapture.

The expression of unstructured intensive experience is crucial to the emergence of creativity, insight, and psychological unfolding. Many mystics of the past have created artistic masterpieces from their intense religious experience. The quality of inspiration is identical for artist and mystic. It is important for creativity within your psychological process as well. If you wish to communicate your mystical experiences to others, verbal creativity is a necessity. Yet how can you communicate that which is beyond words? Once again, we glean a hint from the text of Lambsprinck: rhetoric is that language which is flowery with metaphor. Metaphor is a powerful language that tells us what something is like. It is especially useful for teaching and describing inner experience. Aristotle left us these words:

> The greatest thing by far is to be a master of metaphor; it is the one thing that cannot be learnt from others; and it is also a sign of genius, since a good metaphor implies an intuitive perception of the similarity in the dissimilar.

Metaphorical perception of the mythic dimension of life is a major foundation of Jungian psychology. Through metaphor you learn how your life is "like" the eternal patterns that play themselves eternally through your environment and human behavior. This is an important step in the quest for the Self. We learn to see various myths operating in our personal lives, and participate consciously in our personal mythology.

Metaphorical perception transcends conceptual thinking. Myth raises an individual's awareness to a superhuman or superhistorical plane, enabling access to a higher level of reality than profane existence. The fact that our minds need images to grasp the higher levels of reality suggests that reality is multidimensional and cannot be expressed through intellectual concepts alone.

Myth, says James Hillman, is the comprehensive metaphor, "answering our requirements for intellectual puzzlement, and explanation through enigma by providing as-if fictions in depth, complexity, and exquisite differentiation." "Myth," says Hermann Broch, "is the archetype of every phenomenal cognition of which the human mind is capable. Archetype of all human cognition, archetype of science, archetype of art—myth is consequently that archetype of philosophy, too." We might deduce from this that metaphorical perception is a Jungian artform, and myth functions as a sort of metapsychology.

"The Salamander comes from the fire"

PLATE 10

All legends tell us,
That *the Salamander comes from the fire.*
His food and life are in the fire,
That has been given him as his nature.

His home is in a great mountain,
Round which many fires burn:
The first fire is smaller than the second,
In which the Salamander bathes himself,

And the third is bigger than the second.
In all of these the Salamander washes and bathes all over.

Then he hastens to his burrow,
But on the way he is caught and hooked.
He will soon bleed to death and die.
This regenerates him,
So that he may earn the eternal living God
With his blood; henceforth he can never die.
His blood is the greatest earthly medicine,
You will find nothing to surpass it.

His blood cures all disease
In metals, animals and living men.

From it the Wise draw their mental powers,
And come to God's heavenly gift,
Which is called the Philosopher's Stone,
Changing all to virtue.

The Wise grant it to us with loving hearts,
And on that account we ought to thank them.

The Salamander lives in that fire at rest,
Which makes his color show a most glorious hue.

The repetition, exaltation and improvement of the Tincture, or Philosopher's Stone; it may also be understood as Augmentation.

"The Salamander comes from the fire."

Chapter 10: Mana Personality

The Philosopher's Stone

THE salamander bathes in the hot center of three fires and then retires into his burrow. When he is killed, he bleeds to death but his blood is a great medicine. It is probable that the three fires represent three distinct initiations by fire for the perfecting of the three components of humanity: mind, emotions, and body. In alchemy, fire is the means of transmutation and the instrument for testing purity. If *solutio* corresponds with water, *coagulatio* with earth, and *sublimatio* with air, *calcinatio* completes the elemental quaternity and is attributed to fire. M. L. von Franz interprets the salamander as *prima materia*, roasting in the fiery emotional reactions involved in the process of withdrawing projections.

Fire symbolizes libido or psychic energy. It may come from sexuality. The three trials-by-fire are an image to express three stages in the transformation of consciousness: 1) autoerotic; 2) personal power-seeking; and 3) refined transpersonal consciousness. We can survive the ordeal of fire if we refine our search for our higher Self rather than remain motivated solely by the ego. For you to be psychically "invulnerable" to the fire means that you have become immune to your former tendency to identify with your emotional reactions or those of others.

There is a basic exercise in psychosynthesis that allows you to systematically disidentify from your body, emotions, mind, and contents of consciousness. You affirm that you value each of these, then recognize and affirm that you are a center of pure self-consciousness, a center of will. This expansion of awareness leads to embracing a new, expanded identity. One sacrifice to the fire is the codependent tendency to become over invested in the emotional weather of others. You are no longer caught up in their acting out, caught up by their drama and intense affect.

Ideally this expansion is leading you toward peak experiences, self-actualization, and cosmic consciousness. But you inhabit a purgatory of insecurity and disequilibrium as your old worldview transmutes into the new. You need freedom to experiment with new modes of awareness and ways of being. The salamander hastens to his burrow after refining. In much the same way, creative lifestyle changes incubate quietly within, then suddenly comes the illumination or creative idea. In between, others may mistake your appropriate introversion for depression.

Once you synthesize your new viewpoint on reality, you discover a new sense of well-being and contentment. You can expect many rounds of this same process in life's perpetually changing circumstances. You break out of the old world view, go through the birth canal, and regenerate in a new dimension of awareness. You have a new self-image and many new potentials in life. Each time you go through the cycle you gain awareness and maturity.

Much of this process goes on automatically in your dreams. Your personal growth is tangibly effected when your old self interacts with new states of being that arise spontaneously in dreams. Your new identity comes from both your conscious and subconscious experience, and the shift progresses from emotion to imagery to awareness. Your expanding awareness is in part autonomous.

If you come upon negative images in your dreams, be assured that successfully confronting these, facing your fear and going through it, initiates an expansion of conscious awareness and changes your self image. Positive figures in your dreams often carry the latent aspects of new identity. You may use them as a resource, integrating their characteristics into your actual behavior and identity.

The man attacking and attempting to hook the salamander shows a stance of fighting against the very changes that would lead to increased awareness and fuller life. The uninitiated individual, unaware of what is happening to him, bucks the process of spontaneous change from within. The initiate cooperates and facilitates its development. Once again, dreamwork is an important aspect of the process.

Many things take place beyond the level of conscious awareness, including spontaneous creative activity, but most people suppress it by choosing conformity instead. This conformity consists essentially in identifying with outdated worldviews. But the salamander regenerates despite this struggling ego. Contact with your own inner nature is the panacea for all life's ills. It facilitates drive, personality, soul, and *mana* (or personal power). Simple lack of self-awareness and a negative attitude keep the average person from recognizing it.

After a crisis in development, the expansion of awareness is accomplished in a breakthrough. You easily leave old habits behind and enter a new world of understanding. Dreamwork helps you create a tangible reality from something seemingly unreal. You become sensitive to the automatic process of transformation occurring continually within. Jung originally became interested in alchemy when he noticed the parallel between images in clients' dreams and the process of alchemy. Inner transformation takes place continuously in dreams. They help us adapt and evolve.

In dreams, you can exist in more than one state of being, and this indicates you are in the process of a critical change in your personality, emerging as someone new. What was painful is transforming into something beautiful. When this happens in dreams, it prepares you to experience further mystical states of consciousness. When you make an active effort to facilitate the dreamworld in daily life, you reap the benefit of further expanded awareness and may even experience the faculty of lucid dreaming. The healing effects you experience may spread contagiously from you to others. When you actualize your new state, you are pervaded with feelings of well-being. You can channel this into any form of creativity, but channel it you must.

The refining fire is a variation on the theme of hellfire and purgatory. Psychologically it means that our development is fostered by the frustration of our sensual and power desires, but only if we have a viable channel of communication with our Higher Self. This very frustration is the initiatory ordeal of this phase. With hellfire comes *judgement* after death in many cultures. In one way, judgement is similar to the evaluation of a craftsman in shaping an object to his will. Verdict and execution of sentence are analogous to the blows of the hammer to correct a flaw or defect in the nature of the object worked.

This analogy carries into alchemy. As human beings we are evolving toward perfection, but initiation into the Mysteries is intended to speed our evolution to optimal human potential. The refining fire helps you purge yourself of the desire to use your psychic energy for personal pleasure or power. The refining fire creates an integrated synthesis of your personality by fusing the four elements into a unity, the Philosopher's Stone. Your purged ego allows soul to enter body and spirit to enter soul. The experience is a penetrating divine inspiration.

Sacrifice-to-make-holy (or ego-death of the desire and power nature) is the key factor in the perfecting process. Bathing in the fire-bath of immortality means you make a connection between your ego and the transpersonal psyche. This makes you aware of your own transpersonal, immortal aspect. Through the refinement by fire, you learn to see the archetypal aspect of existence. The fire takes on the transforming aspects of the Holy Spirit, rather than being merely a consuming terrestrial fire that reflects the pain of a frustrated ego.

It is a supreme sacrifice to give up our own lives for the sake of others. If we do this negatively, we fall into the emotional pit of codependence. The positive approach is to realize there are sacrifices at all levels of existence, and finally we must surrender to the will of God, totally without reservation. This presupposes that we can exercise our will, for this is no mere lip service. It requires a correct orientation of your whole being, including the subconscious and superconscious. We often see people with good intentions governed by subconscious complexes; they can't link up their neurosis with the superconscious transforming power. They do not rule their elemental nature like King Sol, but are ruled by it.

We must learn to live in the outer world of matter, but also be a citizen of the inner world. This happens as we come to realize more and more how events originate in the inner and manifest in the outer realm. Sacrifice of self for Self is the great medicine. In the alchemical process, you must create the Philosopher's Stone over and over again. Two extremely important aspects of this process are imagination (soul) and meditation (spirit). As alchemist, you must make many repetitions of your return to the depths before you perfect your art. This requires discipline and consistency.

The stone symbolizes the actualized wisdom and increased understanding that is building within you. The Stone is a union (coniunctio) of Sun and Moon, masculine and feminine, and has its own internal cyclic dynamism. This union of opposites integrates the split-off parts of yourself so you become most truly your Self for the first time. Your unified personality gives equal consideration to all modes of perceiving reality: intuition, thinking, feeling, and sensation.

When your personality is total, you can withdraw your projections from the world and begin to see each other soul for the beauty it is. Your state of wholeness is reflected in increasing synchronistic events, suspending time, space, and causation. Your sense of immortality and sacred space expands. After experiencing unity, you break into a new multiplicity so life can go on.

Imagination is a concentrated extract of the life forces, both physical and psychic. Alchemical literature always obscures whether the ultimate transformation is more in the physical or spiritual world. The soul functions both in the body and through projection in the physical world. Meditation is a spiritual practice that allows soul to become open and receptive to the union of masculine and feminine potential. It makes absolutely no difference which gender you are; the process is the same.

The salamander of this illustration bathes in the central fire which is the life force responsible for germination and growth in nature. The salamander is mysteriously not consumed by the fire and thereby reveals itself as yet another form of the original primal substance. As the alchemist, you concentrate on the inner world, and generate libido or psychic energy, which is symbolized by the fire. This fire nourishes the salamander, and treating the tincture with this fire augments its power.

Your ego-complex carries within it the potential for oneness and wholeness of your personality. But, before this potential can be realized, you must first make some effort to increase personal awareness, perhaps by concentrating on a dream or sitting in meditation. Then, to the extent that you realize the Self, it becomes part of your conscious personality. Your soul lives on images and metaphor. Let the image come into your body. As you embrace the image, you embrace the feminine. Find your special relationship to metaphor.

The Self is like your *inner child*, which nourishes itself and grows like the salamander in the fire of emotion. Your emotions may have been frozen or numbed during childhood trauma and even through later events. To the extent you have done your emotional clearing, you will have reclaimed your frozen feelings and all the lost or abandoned parts of yourself. This is experienced largely through image, whereby mind, imagination, and feeling, come together in a multisensory experience.

Emotional catharsis or breakthrough combines masculine and feminine energies. The pain you feel as you get close to unresolved issues turns up the psychic heat, more and more, until you surrender to the process. Your awareness of the important activities of the Self increases. The Self extracts life from the fire. This means it becomes ever-more saturated with libido. This energy charge keeps building until your inner personality finds unity and the Self permeates all activities of your conscious being.

Amazingly, this salamander-child has the emergent capacity of curing sick people! Your healthy presence becomes a general medicine as the outer effects of the Stone are multiplied. In other words, if you are truly individuated, you can trigger off the same process in other people. This is because when a person meets someone whose worldview is more expansive, their limitations automatically begin to dissolve. Through contact with a whole person's worldview, new possibilities become obvious.

The shaman is the archetype of wounded-healer and is perceived as having much *mana* or personal power for healing and vision. In today's society, the shaman-therapist functions in much the same way. It is impossible to practice therapy without first having worked through your own issues, your own wounds. Doing therapy on someone else will bring them up if they are unresolved.

The contagious effect of the Self is the whole basis for "willing of the power" from one individual to another in an initiatory school. It is a transferral of structured self-integration. Outside of a spiritual school, the less deliberate actions of an adept are often most effective. In this way other people get pulled into the healing process. This is the sense of "when the student is ready, the teacher appears." Synchronicities, or meaningful coincidences, multiply. More and more you sense your unity with cosmos, with the universal.

Suddenly, everything seems to be in synch, flowing exactly as it is supposed to for using connections and tensions for growth. Recognizing the spontaneous manifestation of archetypal patterns in your personal life evokes deep emotional feelings. In that moment you are one with that archetype in an epiphany of conscious realization. But it is an experience in sacred and not profane time, so the ego makes no grab for glory. You simply experience the immediate perception of "I Am That." Only then do you tap into the vital renewing power of the archetype. This is the basis of invocation.

When you experience an archetype in this fundamental way, you create a whole new situation for yourself. A new pattern crystallizes and emerges. When the correspondences between the objective and subjective take place, a new pattern is set up in time. This pattern is not capable of being anticipated in terms of cause and effect. These patterns appear spontaneously, due to the activation of archetypes within your psyche. The crucial motivating factor is an internal ordering principle, the dynamic Self.

Archetypes, like images and dreams, have a holographic quality. In a hologram any one part enfolds the whole, therefore the whole can be reconstructed from any part. Keying into any aspect of an archetype opens up the possibility of a wide range of experience and can lead to deep healing. Some of it will always remain in potential, even while you unfold or actualize that part of it which is your personal destiny. Images, dreams, and archetypes all reveal more meaning over time than we could possibly extract from them at any given moment of our life. The understanding contained in any type of symbol or dream is always more than that which can be known. Synchronicity influences the unfolding of the pattern when your objective and subjective realities unite.

There are clusters of images and symbols which all relate to a given archetype. Corresponding colors, plants, astrological signs, scents, gems, and animals point to specific archetypal patterns at work in our inner and outer environment. For example; yellow, heliotrope, sunflower, the sign Leo, lion, frankincense, and diamond all correspond with the archetype of the Sun. Through perceiving the frequency of these images in your dreams, fantasies, and environment you learn to see specific archetypes and their characteristic patterns and myths at work in your personal life. There are several of these basic patterns of unfoldment in the psyche. The Self forms a unifying matrix for all archetypal patterns. The Self is, in fact, the quintessential archetype and the primary symbol of the individuation process.

The Self is the ultimate purpose behind both the impersonal archetypes that manifest and the archetypal process by which the ego and consciousness emerge. The Self expresses essence and aim. In other words, the "aim" and "essence" is the awareness of the Self. You may recall that the word "sin" was originally an archery term for "missing the mark." Where are you "missing the mark" and denying your Self?

True knowledge of yourself is the knowledge of the objective psyche as it manifests in dreams and other subconscious imagery. To meditate on this is an effort toward self-knowledge. This is not necessarily in the interest of the ego, but lends some objectivity in answering the question, "Who am I?" A good psychosynthesis exercise is simply to make a list of answers to this self-posed question: "Who am I?" Another is to meditate on your breath, periodically asking yourself, "Who is aware?" You can observe your consciousness, and observe yourself observing, ad infinitum until there is no separation and no difference. No doer and no watcher remains.

The key is to find the meaning of life from one second to the next. This meaning is the basis for immortality—that mortal state in which you constantly enjoy the presence of divinity. Another exercise is to begin dialogue with your higher Self in your journal, receiving answers from the unconscious. In this case, let the dialogue flow spontaneously from within once you have relaxed your body and mind.

Alchemists believe that, with the help of God, we can create an immortal or glorified body to inhabit after natural death. The Chinese have an equivalent yoga exercise for creating what they term the *diamond body*. It requires a voluntary diminishing of the bright light of solar-consciousness to allow the repressed feminine back in. This allows the unconscious to flow through us without self-consciously concentrating on it. This is an absolute reversal of the beginning stage of the *Opus*, or Great Work.

The Philosopher's Stone symbolizes something like concrete or actualized wisdom. Projection means that when the alchemist has made the elixir or stone, he throws it on other objects which are thereby perfected, or turned into gold. This gold is a realization of their inherent spiritual value and meaning.

The Self conveys to the ego the characteristics of reliable stability which makes ego less susceptible to regressively "falling apart." Experiences of the Self have an eternal, timeless, or ancient quality. They create an experience of sacred time and space. To be in contact with the Self brings awareness of transpersonal meaning, above your day-to-day milieu. This is symbolized in the next plate as conversation with the Guardian Angel. This is an on-going dialogue with the Self.

Awareness of the Self and a requirement for the total personality eliminate the conditions under which split-off complexes can survive. This unified personality gives equal consideration to the main aspects of life: intuition (fire); thinking (air); feeling (water); and sensation (earth). There is unification of the elemental nature; physical (earth), emotional (water), mental (air), and spiritual (fire). All four planes of existence are united in the original state of wholeness, now regained on a level of conscious realization.

With the advent of self-realization, the tyranny of the egotistical identity is over. The Hindu word for egoism happens to be *mana*. This eastern term includes conceit, arrogance, and pride. It implies comparing one's own qualities with those of another and emerging the winner. Hindus are cautioned that this haughtiness should be considered like a madness. This potential negative aspect of *mana* or social power only occurs if the individual identifies with the archetypal dynamism and becomes vainglorious. Sometimes this is a subtle process, and difficult to detect in oneself.

There is a tendency in the helping professions for people to consider themselves "healers." There is another analogy to the salamander being caught and hooked, and subsequently bleeding to death. There are nowadays directories in most cities of alternative health practitioners. Generally more kinds of therapy than you could imagine will be represented. From body work, to crystal healing, to channeling, breathwork, naturopathic medicine, rebirthing, ghostbusting, to transformational psychology, and more. The articles in these directories speak of myth and magic and hold the promise of answers that are still a mystery to you.

Each of these healers has differing training and credentials, but all are offering up their special wisdom, the healing balm. They are thus likely to capture and contain the projections of others. Their unique personalities act as a "hook" for archetypal projections. For the dependent, it is their task to carry that projection for a while, until the client can re-own it and develop a relationship to the inner healer. It is, in fact, this inner healer that truly does all the regenerative work in therapy. The therapist simply helps the client access it. But it is the responsibility of the therapist not to kill the projection prematurely, for that is murderous to the soul.

The client comes to know that all the healing resources are within and finds empowerment. His or her responsibility is to formulate questions consciously. In this way, the unconscious is mobilized, maybe through dream, or just knowing the answer. Whenever you can formulate a question, your unconscious has the capacity to answer. This is the basis of all forms of divination, from the *I Ching* to the Tarot to channeling. If you are a so-called healer, you must be careful not to take the credit for yourself, but realize it is the archetype working through you. This sometimes is trickier to accomplish than you may think.

A solution is to give credit where credit is due, by maintaining your own dialogue with the ultimate *mana* figures that trace back to the Wise Old Man and Great Mother. The masculine wisdom figure is the archetype of *Spirit*, while the wise woman embodies *Matter*. Both figures can appear in projections, dreams, and imagination in a multitude of forms, but all exert a powerful fascination over us. If we identify with them we fall prey to self-glorification and megalomania. Others will be certain to project from time to time. The reputations of alternative health practitioners and therapists are built on word of mouth about their powers, and abilities, and healing success.

Clients want the balm of their soothing care, the clarity of their vision, and power of their healing force. You need simply avoid getting caught up in your own growing legend. Be careful never to foster dependency in your clients, and don't act like a cult leader. Personality cults were rampant with the channeling fad. Now, thankfully, people are more interested in connecting with their Higher Self. But we saw many examples of what happens to those who identify with or exploit the *mana* personality.

Mana belongs in the primal sense to the two archetypal *mana* personalities. Jung defined *mana* as an extraordinary power or pure energy. Someone with *mana* has the means of having power over others, especially social power. This person, so invested, emanates charisma. When you experience yourself having a potent catalytic effect on others there is usually some ego inflation, which is paradoxically a regression into unconsciousness. Jung said everyone succumbs to it for a while in the course of the deep inward journey. Then more insights come, and you learn to humbly distinguish yourself from the god and goddess within. *Mana* initiates the mystic as a spiritual child of God; socially, *mana* initiates the religious process.

The concept of *mana* has been with us since ancient times in all cultures. Under many names philosophers, scientists, and mystics have referred to it time and again. Whether known as *chi*, *prana*, animal magnetism, universal energy, Odic force, orgon, psi faculty, or *wakonda*, it is all essentially the same. This all-pervading vital force has the power of growth and magic healing that is generally called *mana*.

Magical healing is generally the province of shamans, magicians, the sorceress. They are neither good nor bad, but always intense. Their ability to heal, their *mana*, comes from the fact that they have suffered their own wounding and recovery. Shamans characteristically suffer a schizophrenic breakdown of personality, but find a way out of their dilemma and acquire the ability to heal others. They initiate the same process of inner healing through charisma, spiritual strength, integrity, and authority. Verbal magic is especially effective in penetrating the other person. It is startling to see the impact of one person creating awe in another.

This experience of *mana* is the root of both magical and religious experience. *Mana* itself is an impersonal force, like electricity. However, it attaches to some individuals, and manifests in results. If you have it, you can use it, but it can occur anywhere spontaneously. Those with conspicuous success display *mana*. The more *mana*, the greater the impression and the influence. *Mana* underlies religion and magic.

You may come closer to the pure *mana* personalities by clearing your father-complex and mother-complex. We all suffer parental wounding, which manifests as neurosis. No parent can supply all the emotional needs of a child or be the godlike figure the child projects. If the parents are our original wound, that which wounded us can also parent us. These wounds give birth to our destiny.

Self-reparenting means giving thirty minutes daily to listening to the needs of your inner child of the past, so he or she can be fully present with you now. An open wound is a symbol of immaturity; when healing emerges from a wound's depth, it leaves a scar. The scar unites the opposites of softness and hardness, weakness and strength. The scar reminds of tender places. The wounded healer unites male and female, body and soul.

The modern healer is moving away from identification with the heroic mode with its epic, historical orientation toward imaginative fantasy. Awareness is growing that image-consciousness heals. You may sense your life as a dynamic image: your dream life, behavior fantasies, sex fantasies, social mask, etc. Religion and old-fashioned therapies forced standardized healing images on people. Now, those who choose to foster the soul-spirit reunion are learning to facilitate the image emerging from within.

In terms of mystical experience, this is the perception of *pure energy* of a universal nature. You can experience it as a surge of power, a feeling of letting go, or an intense experience of light. You might perceive it as increased efficiency in your social power, recognition, charisma. At first these sensations will come and go suddenly and unexpectedly. This stage of pure energy may occur spontaneously if you are unprepared. But, if you have been meditating, this stage may be actively induced. It brings a feeling of a subtle form of energy that is spiritual in nature.

This pure energy is most properly used to construct a new mystical body of this fine substance. If not channeled into this highest goal, it may "leak out" as *siddhas* or magical powers. These are uniformly shunned in Eastern systems of meditation. The Western system of theurgic magic would only condone using the building power to recycle into further aspiration. Meditation provides the balancing required.

The basic symbolism of the yogic quest through meditation is analogous with a magician's initiation. Both "die" to fleshly pleasures. Both then ascend to heaven. The aspirant is reborn with a new spiritual body. He is dismembered and remembered as he sunders one earthly appetite after another. Ascending to heaven he acquires divine powers.

The ultimate yogic goal is to enter *samadhi,* a mystical state similar to that of the magician-initiate who is able to live the sacred symbolism of his society literally. He has become the temple. This literal experience of symbolism in turn confers upon him magical powers, though orthodox yogis renounce them. Yoga originated from shamanism and primitive magic. Freedom, or exemption from social forms, was originally a magician's prerogative.

To escape invasion by the *mana* personality, we need to be aware of its awe-inspiring effect in our lives. Through therapy, self-discovery, and process theology we open our consciousness to our internal psychic processes. Through mysticism, we learn how to carry on with that same process in a dimension that includes our deepest depths. The *mana* personality lies very close to the center of the psyche, the Self. Nevertheless, as your ego seeks to assimilate unconscious contents, inflation will follow with an exaggerated sense of your capacity and potentiality. Time and again you will have to distinguish yourself from the god and goddess within. It isn't just an "inner" experience, since the impact of experience in either world pervades the other.

As you spiral in toward the Self you feel the new freedom of being relatively complex-free. You feel an energy release, expanded awareness, and feel uninhibited. But this very sense of power and "enlightenment" is the counterbalancing return into unconsciousness. You may be a can-do person of action and a sagacious counselor, or just plain *full-of-it.* Your detractors will quickly notice your limitations. *Mana* also manifests as grace, and this saving grace can help you take yourself a little less seriously. The *mana* personality is a godlike person, but heaven help one who goes around acting like God Almighty!

"Father, Son, and Guide hold each other's hand"

PLATE 11

An Old Father has come
From fair Israel. He has an only Son,
Whom he loves with all his heart.

He is filled with sorrow,
For a guide is decreed to lead his Son
To whatever goal he asks or wills.

The Guide speaks thus to the Son:
"Come, I will lead you everywhere,
High to a summit on a mountain peak,
That you may learn to know all the world,
From there you can watch the earth and the great seas,
So you may be well pleased.
Then I will lead you into the Sky
Until we come to Heaven's towers."

The Son is glad at the words of the Guide,
And immediately climbs up with him;

There he is shown the splendor of Heaven's throne,
Created beautiful in all things.

But now he has seen it,
He sighs for his Father.
He laments his Father's great sorrow,
Wishing that he was once more on his Father's bosom.

Father, Son, and Guide hold each other's hand,
Body, Spirit, Soul; you should understand.

"Father, Son, and Guide hold each other's hand."

Chapter 11: Puer/Senex

Magical Child

THIS plate reveals a quantum leap in consciousness. In former plates the only human figures were solitary portrayals of the ego, unregenerate or regenerate. Now three powerfully distinct characters emerge, each with their different perspective, but harmonizing. Each of these symbols, on its own, is a classical symbol of the Self: the King, the Prince, and the Angel. Lambsprinck informs us that his process knows them as body, spirit, and soul. The amazing thing is that the Angel, as soul-guide, is offering him an experience of transcendence. The offer is eagerly accepted, until the yearning for the body returns to claim his awareness.

Plate 11 illustrates the first in a series of distillation processes. The Old King represents matter, for God the Father is the creator of the universe, in alchemical philosophy. The interplay of matter, or nature, is his mantle. This interplay at the threshold of manifestation is continual. As light coalesces into matter, and matter etherealizes into light, it is impossible to tell the difference between particle and wave. In any event, our nuclear constituents may be seen as a form of frozen light or spirit. Billions of years ago, our atomic elements cooked in the heart of some giant sun. The background of the plate is still Mother Earth, who as an entity stands in close relationship to mankind. She sustains our life, even though we ultimately give up our bodies to her.

The young Prince is the spirit. The spirit from one point of view is a child of Earth. It is only able to operate and control material conditions through its physical body provided by the Earth. However, the spirit has a real existence independent of the transitory world of phenomenal existence. Spirit, as a dynamic, tends to move out of time, space, matter, and causation toward transcendence. You probably know people caught up in their spiritual practice who would rather stay in the celestial heights than come back down to earth.

The guide is the soul, depicted with wings much like the goddess Psyche who has butterfly wings. This spirit guide looks like an angel whose task it is to intermediate between heaven and earth. This guide represents the interplay between matter and spirit, the degree of their interaction. The soul truly has wings that will take it to the heights. It is old and wise, and for this reason has its feet firmly planted on the ground. In the biblical dream of Jacob's ladder, he saw many angels moving in between sky above and earth below. These angels represent the ascents and descents of the soul, distilling the essence of the individual.

These are the three constituents of the process of human evolution, seen from alchemy's perspective. As an individual evolves, the Spirit is attracted toward its heavenly origin. In so doing it tends to neglect a primary purpose of human life: experience of the discipline of the material body. Instead we try to enforce a human sense of order on the physical world through science and psychology. What we need to develop is a balanced personality that can experience discreet transcendence through meditation daily.

When your consciousness and life are engaged in time, you become transparent to transcendence. In the text, the guide alludes to an elevated perspective which allows observation of both land and seas. This indicates that your maturing spirituality has insight into both conscious and unconscious processes. You may not find immediate enlightenment, but there is more light in your life.

The King has a sense of itself as a limited being bound to the planet. This King knows it cannot evolve to maturity and equilibrium without the help of the spirit. Some days we may feel earth-bound or world-weary and long for the heights of a peak experience to raise us to another plane of awareness. It is only through contact with the spirit that the body/mind achieves nominal existence. That which is beyond is theoretically unknowable through the senses. Some people feel that spiritual contact is easier at certain sacred sites on the earth, and sacred mountains rank high among the preferred destinations.

As a spiritual being, you have a duty to your physical vehicle that cuts to the core of your identity. How can you both respect your body and honor your transcendent, intuitive, and imaginative self? You learn to apply discrimination in every situation affecting the physical body and matter in general. Perhaps you make a commitment to recycling, preserving the environment, or lobbying against nuclear power.

You come to realize deeply that your actions have repercussions outside of their apparent scope. Perhaps we can't all be artists, healers, sages, or saints, but we can do our parts individually and make a collective impact. Do you treat your body like a King in terms of giving it quality food, proper rest, and eliminating self-destructive behavior? This personal ecology spreads from within out into social and planetary concern.

You can enter any of the Lambsprinck pictures as if you were entering your own dream fragment. Allow yourself to experience each of the primary figures of the plate. Let yourself become that king, that prince, and that guide. What do you feel, and what do you have to say as that aspect of existence? After exploring the figures, you may want go even deeper into the gestalt, by identifying with less obvious aspects such as the earth, water, or sky. You may even amplify your personal meaning for the castle-keep or discover what could happen in the boat floating on the water. There are deeper mysteries here than could ever be fully unraveled.

On the psychological level, the soul stands between the opposites of father and son as the reconciling factor. In Jungian psychology the development of masculine consciousness is linked to the *puer* and *senex* archetypes: *puer* means "boy" and equates with the Young Prince; *senex* means "old man" and is the Old King. *Senex*, as the body, represents the fettered conditions of limited human nature. His temperament is cold, his attitudes realistic or pragmatic. The *senex* embodies awareness through the senses. He is practical and methodical. He symbolizes terminal conditions of entropy, such as order, fulfillment, perfection, and death.

An archetype, the *senex* fostered your budding ego-formation as a child through the father-image. This father encourages disciplined routine but also indicates that habitual behavior pattern that persists past its prime. By keeping an individual trapped in a rut, it can exert an inhibiting influence. Disguising itself as the good old Puritan work ethic, it can make sure you have no time left for spiritual practice. *Senex* manifests in your dreams as father, mentor, wise old man, or teacher. He represents authority, wisdom, and guidance that is beyond your own personal maturity. But he can make you intolerant of your own youthful folly or frivolity.

The *senex* affects creative contemplation of the ultimate meaning of fate. He is the character who classically induces depression or melancholia. But the most extreme negative attitudes can only dominate you if the *senex* is split from your *puer* aspect. The father-son split can be acted out with your parent, your body, your emotions, your thoughts, and spiritual discipline. As a positive virtue, *senex* as wise old man is a transformed continuation of the *puer*. A mature personality has a very earthy kind of spirituality, which is well-grounded and disciplined. He is not at odds with his youthful aspirations, but has integrated them into a creative spiritual life. To the extent that is humanly possible, youthful ideals are incorporated into a lifestyle.

The *puer*, or eternal adolescent in us, represents the spirit as the divine child. This archetype of a miraculous child is a symbol of promise. He is the star of our visions of new being and represents our spiritual potential. His appearance as a symbol anticipates future developments, or changes in your personality. The divine child is a very potent symbol that represents the synthesis of conscious and unconscious elements of the personality. This final synthesis has not yet taken place, but he intimates that the healing process is going on at a deeper level. In his negative aspect, the *puer* indicates retarded psychological development rather than new beginnings. This mindset is apparent in the Peter Pan type who refuses to grow up.

Jung noted a growing increase in *puer* psychology after World War II. This trend bloomed with the Flower Children, peace movement, and psychedelic era. Idealistic baby boomers are now coming into greater political power and only beginning to implement some of the idealistic notions that took root in the sixties and seventies. Many of these people have become socially conscious, responsible adults. Others, however, fell along the wayside to drugs, misunderstood spiritual emergency, and disenchantment.

One typical *puer* pattern was to go "back to the land," then when finances got tight to escape into fantasy through drinking or drugs. Clarion calls of the *puer* were "Don't trust anyone over thirty!" and "Die young and leave a good-looking corpse." These unfortunate *puer* souls failed to realized they could complete the process of ego-death within without having to self-destruct the body.

Puer/senex is a continuum of consciousness. As with any archetypal dyad, there is danger when an individual approaches one isolated polar extreme. But even if you see *puer* psychology dominating your life, or someone else's, be careful about making a "diagnosis" that this *puer* is a pathological condition. It is difficult to know how the spirit is moving this soul. Some of us need to outgrow the *puer*; yet others need to grow by means of *puer* psychology and experience. Their lessons come through experiencing this archetypal mode. The *puer* of Lambsprinck's work seems to be a youth just emerging into manhood, still eagerly building knowledge and awareness of the world.

The *puer* is a variant on the archetypal theme of Divine or *Magical Child*. A child symbolizes something evolving toward independence. The independence it seeks is the separation from the conflict situation of conscious and unconscious positions. The conscious mind is unable to achieve this; therefore, the child symbol appears showing the newly conceived state of consciousness. In chemistry, a *nascent state* is the uncombined condition of an atom in its most active state, at the moment of its liberation from a compound. This opens the potential of recombining in a new way.

The child, as Spirit, is ultimately a bringer of light and enlarger of consciousness. The urge or compulsion for self-realization is a law of nature and thus carries invincible power. This compulsive urge gets mixed up with self-destruction and results in the myriad of toxic behaviors. But in recovery, this spiritual yearning shows through. It is the potential for a new personality, a new life. In the beginning, the child is insignificant or improbable, like the Philosopher's Stone. Nevertheless, the child grows strong, and its miraculous power is revealed as time goes on.

This symbol of the Self (Son) arises in the depths of the body (Father), expressing its materiality. Seen in this way, the symbol is a living body, and the child is a totally appropriate representation of the symbolic content. The child, like the *prima materia*, symbolizes both the beginning and end of the Great Work (*ultima materia*). Thus your archetypal child within, that magical child, shows both your pre-conscious and post-conscious essence. This special child symbolizes both beginning and end, much like Christ calling himself the *Alpha* and *Omega*. The Self, as wholeness, is both older and younger than consciousness and transcends it in time and space.

Your psychic life precedes your consciousness and anticipates future significant developments. These manifest in dreams, intuitions, divinations, psychic phenomena, and the symbols of futurity in your unfolding process. If you are male, or working with *animus* issues as female, the appearance of the child with the father shows an equilibrated path of masculine development. The best qualities of both the old and new are becoming harmonized through the natural process of maturation.

For a woman, or a man reconnecting with femininity, the child is an inherent aspect of futurity. We can all come into awareness of the eternal feminine within bearing the divine child. This is the central feminine mystery and secret purpose of cyclic transformation. She must carry the spirituality that comes upon her as a visitation of God. The child aspect is in a special relationship with the transcendent spiritual powers of the collective unconscious. *Puer* impulses are messages or calls from the spirit.

Have you ever had the feeling that your soul was "pregnant" with the spiritual potential for greater awareness? If so, how was this child conceived? This miraculous child will appear spontaneously in your imagery in advance of a major transformation in your psyche. When the child appears barely developed, the changes are embryonic but have vast potential for growth.

This archetype is the divinity within our immature striving and our unconscious limitations. In the initial stages of any process, the potential is always fuller than any limited realization. The divine child has a capacity to mature into a cultural hero or *mana* personality. And this is what we see in Lambsprinck's depiction. He is moving into regal maturity aided by the gentle guiding of the Self.

Watch your dreams for images of a special or precocious child. What changes in your qualitative behavior could this child foreshadow? What qualities do you find emerging and want to stabilize? Also watch for handicapped, sick, or dying children. Perhaps you can imaginaly nurse them back to health and grow up a potential which might have been abandoned, cut off, or distorted. The divine child also carries forward the spiritual heritage of your ancestors. Socially, the child carries our aspirations and utopian ideals.

Do not confuse this child with your inner recovering child. It probably won't present a personality like the *anima-animus*. It is not your own any more than your parents are Great Mother and Wise Old Man. It just symbolizes the miraculous renewal of life, new potentials, and new beginnings. As this magical child matures, you overcome many difficulties and develop your own sense of meaning and a lifestyle that expresses that meaning. At the appropriate time the divine child manifests the dynamic change it formerly symbolized. Then it dies back into the collective having accomplished its purpose.

Negatively, this child often indicates emotional development stunted in adolescence. Ask this image about developments that are still immature, but have the potential for growth and change. A typical negative *puer* symbol might be a male or female punk or heavymetal type, alone or in a gang.

Puer is characteristically idealistic, narcissistic, highly sexualized, androgynous, inspiring, and inventive. It can be a burning impulse for creativity or destruction. *Puer* is the motivator of "life in the fast lane." Fiery youth flies high and fast toward self-destructive burnout, like Icarus. When unbalanced tendencies get the upper hand, *puer* can lead to a car accident, plane crash, any death at high speed.

That speed may be metaphorical and manifest as addiction to amphetamines or cocaine. When the pattern of negativity get strong enough, it is the syndrome of *puer aeternus*, the personality stuck in adolescent psychology. Then you find someone who is impatient, wants immediate gratification, indulges in high-flying fantasies, is an adrenalin junkie, and revels in frequent ego-trips. Irresponsibility and lack of ability for intimacy and commitment are also present.

Puer has a tendency to wander, or travel aimlessly. The pattern of *puer aeternus* mirrors the myth or theme of the child god Iacchus or Bacchus of the Eleusinian mysteries. This god of fragmentation, or psychic dissociation and renewal, is also the god of intoxication and appears in patterns of addiction, especially where alcoholism or drug addiction are the main life themes. Iacchus is also a god associated with bisexuality.

Puella aeterna is the feminine counterpart. She is a high-flyer type who is reckless, impulsive, and vacillating. She is a perennial flirt. She behaves like a sister with her children, rather then parenting them in a mature way, focusing on their needs. But *puer* and *puella* also embody spontaneity, enthusiasm, and seemingly limitless energy. They bring us new solutions, revolutionary ideas unbound by past tradition or convention.

Grandiose dreams and schemes come from *puer*, the herald of new beginnings. But sober judgement, organization, and management are needed to bring schemes to fruition. *Puer* tends to "space off" into fantasy fulfillment and lacks a sense of materiality, corporeality, or substance. *Puer* is the archetypal "pipe dreamer." Still, through *puer's* dreaming and wandering we may "find ourselves" and move through our hang-ups.

If the *puer/senex* archetype is split within, you repeatedly engage in actions without consideration of consequences, or fail to act on your knowledge. The split is reflected in the generation gap: youth vs. old age, revolution vs. status quo. The *puer* issues come up again in midlife crisis, trying to recapture youth through a fast car or new lover. If possession by *puer* results in ego inflation, possession by the *senex* brings cynicism, pessimism, depression, hardness of heart, and the encrustations of habit. The therapeutic key is to find the midpoint where the archetype shows its identity as two faces looking in opposite directions. Your ego needs a balanced, healthy model to fulfill its basic functions of self-continuity and self-identity. By affirming your *puer* spirit with its lofty ideals you move quickly toward the *senex* virtues of order and responsibility. Do not forget your youthful idealism. Give it a place in your life and let it move out into society. Your *puer* impulses gain substance and body when rounded out through your history.

The paradoxes of mysticism show the *puer/senex* influence. The mystic quest consists of systematically "rising" through a series of planes of awareness, which are hierarchically arranged. This continuum may be called the "mystic mountain," the planes of existence, seven heavens, etc. *Puer/senex* personifies this continuum of spiritual development and corresponds with a disciplined spiritual quest for mystical experience. This development is realized in varying degrees by those who undertake the task. The day-to-day sense of temporal continuity, the basis of order and the ego, is shown for the illusion it is by the experience of eternal patterns.

The alchemist makes quantum leaps into chaos, into the unknown, like the Fool in the Tarot. This *puer* foolishness, impulsivity, and capriciousness leads to the spontaneous realization of unpredictable and discontinuous events. *Puer* dives enthusiastically into chaos and brings up gifts of the soul, little treasures unearthed from the depths. The alchemist sustains an on-going dialogue with himself. *"Who am I?"* provides a basis for self-reflection and self-awareness.

Puer is the questioner; *senex* answers; then you question your answer, cynically doubting your own self-evaluation until you receive validation from the depths. The experimental and experiential models are crucial. Further experiments lead to transformation and unfolding of the meaning of your personal existence. Ultimately the alchemist becomes the Stone, which is paradoxically a *diamond body* of immortality, and the sense of discovery within every moment. The eternal youth gives you a sense of something to look forward to in life.

The alchemist turns to the Guide for his inner direction. He is the Holy Guardian Angel. Each message from our depths may be viewed as an angel sent to us from God. The angel precedes the words that carry it into consciousness. The symbol precedes the understanding of a concept of entry into a new stage of life. Meaning precedes the language used for conceptualization.

Jung asserted that the eternal child in us "is an indescribable experience, an incongruity, a handicap, and a divine prerogative; an imponderable that determines the ultimate worth or worthlessness of a personality." It all depends if we accept the *puer* challenge and take up the quest or lazily identify with the *puer* when we have become too old for this behavior to be appropriate. Then we are only an aging "rebel without a cause" rather than self-actualizing potential divinity.

In daily life, the *puer* spirit gives you the courage to dream your dreams and see your projects through, even if they have not yet been recognized as meaningful by society at large. When you express your inner images through dance, music, graphic arts, or whatever, you give them life and free your creative spirit. In terms of art therapy, your level of skill matters little. In fact, you may wish to use your nondominant hand to create from the child within.

You may feel a great power emanating from your painting, writing, or other self-expression. You may still be technically immature in its execution. Your work may be unrecognized, but that does not make it worthless, unless you judge it strictly from a crusty *senex* point of view. If you do this, you may become discouraged about your creative growth and become stagnant.

If you seek excellence in any human endeavor or art form, it is important to combine the talent, inventiveness, and revolutionary spirit of the *puer* with the tradition, discipline, consensus evaluation, and perseverance of the *senex*. Then you will excel at the most important task of becoming that which you truly are, most perfectly. In the spiritual quest, your character becomes your medium, and its refining is a perpetual process.

In the process of giving body to your spirituality you are respecting the *senex* "materiality." In "The Psychology of the Child Archetype," Jung realized a truth that spans from the spiritual world to the physical:

> The symbols of the self arise in the depths of the body and they express its materiality every bit as much as the structure of the perceiving consciousness. *The symbol is thus a living body;* hence the child is such an apt formula for the symbol. The uniqueness of the psyche can never enter wholly into reality, it can only be realized approximately, though it still remains the absolute basis of consciousness. The deeper layers of the psyche lose their individual uniqueness as they retreat farther and farther into the darkness. "Lower down," that is to say, as they approach the autonomous functional systems, they become increasingly collective until they are universalized and extinguished in the *body's materiality*, i.e. chemical substances. The body's carbon is simply carbon. Hence, at bottom, the psyche is simply "world." The more archaic and deeper, that is the more physiological, the symbol is, the more collective and universal, the more material it is. The more abstract, differentiated, and specific it is, and the more its nature approximates to conscious uniqueness and individuality, the more it sloughs off its universal character.

Images are representations of your spiritual condition. Images as metaphor bring together body and soul. It is important to your spiritual life to accomplish the reunion of soul and body, because you must be embodied before you can receive spirit. Soul is the receiver. The power of the spirit can not be received until consciousness, the light in matter, is in the body. The first conscious experiences of this integration of body, soul, and spirit are certainly uplifting.

As humans, we all have the possibility of having spontaneous peak experiences. This is a direct impression of the realm of Being. When we first have occasional, uncontrollable mystic ecstasies, they appear as transcendence of our former, more mundane awareness. But with meditation practice this condition can become a plateau from which we normally operate. The mystical self becomes synonymous with the actualized self. A big part of this process has to do with surrender and grace.

All self-actualization does not manifest as peak experience. Among individuals, there are "peakers" and "non-peakers." Finding oneself, or one's center, is a self-actualization which requires breakthroughs, but not necessarily "peaking." Other terms associated with peak experience include *samadhi*, *satori*, rebirth, rapture, transcendental consciousness, and cosmic consciousness.

A peak experience may come to you unpredictably. Sometimes they are triggered by intense sensory experiences, sending you into an exaltation through music, sex, or the awesome beauty of nature. This feeling comes over you suddenly and unexpectedly. If you are afraid of change, or the unfamiliar, you may push the feeling away and never seek to recover it; it may seem overwhelming.

On the other hand, you may welcome it, and encourage its repetition. Peak experiences, reached through a conscious process of self-development or spiritual discipline, are the crowning jewel of the process. It feels very positive in a transcendent way. For the unprepared soul, it may come as a big shock. The soul can be likened to a silk scarf resting on a thorny rosebush. If it is ripped away there can be suffering and damage; if carefully detached prior to ascent, it comes away whole.

Mystic ecstasy is only the first phase of mind expansion. We have the potential of becoming conscious of all space, all time, and the transpersonal dimension. Meditation teaches us access to these realms of experience at will. Not every individual feels this state as an ecstasy; for some it seems more like inspiration.

The initial mystical state is a response experience where you feel a sense of Presence, but do not hear or see the Higher Power. It is the lowest of the psychedelic (mind-expanding) stages. Its effects include a purification of the self, vanishing of fear, shame, and guilt, realization that "all is One," and a sense of brotherhood with all life. Sometimes this level is felt as a merging with nature. In all experiences of this level there is a *feeling of oneness with the creation, but not the creator.*

Meditation may still be an effort at this stage, since it has not yet become habitual. Periods of minor, spontaneous peak experience need to be followed up by disciplined action and development for further progress. Peak experiences are a glimpse of what is available in the future—*they symbolize potential, not accomplishment.*

At this phase God is veiled by nature or other imagery. These peak experiences are more emotional than mental in their effect. They tend to occur outside of any time you may devote to meditation, rather than during concentration. You *feel* the presence of God.

"The Son speaks to his Guide"

PLATE 12

Here *the Son speaks to his Guide;*
"I will now return to my Father,
For he can neither live nor act without me."

The Guide immediately answers the Son;
"I will not let you go down alone;
I have led you from your Father's bosom,
And I must bring you there again,
That he may once more rejoice in life
With the virtue we will bring to him."

They both stood up and started off,
Returning to the Father's presence.

When the Father saw the son,
He rose up and cried:

This high peak of India lies in a vessel;
Guide and Son, Soul and Spirit, have climbed to the skies.

"The Son speaks to his Guide."

Chapter 12: Transcendent Function

Self or God-Image

THIS plate represents a further phase in the process of distillation. Here the Soul leads the Spirit to the peak of a high mountain where the Sun and Moon shine on them simultaneously. That is the unification of opposites. Spirit is separated from matter and is exalted with the guidance of the Soul. The Soul, depicted as an Angel, represents the transcendent function, the transmuting power of the symbol. During this phase, you experience a heightened sense of yourself and the world.

Your consciousness enjoys or surveys a larger domain. You become more circumspect. The transcendent function unifies and includes all the functions of consciousness—thinking, feeling, sensation, intuition—within itself; it is known as the fifth function, the quintessence. Working with images you get your head, heart, gut, and psychism participating in unification, even if only for moments, then you bring those realizations back into normal awareness, back into the body.

Symbols stand for what you don't yet know consciously. All the symbols and archetypal figures in which the process is embodied are vehicles of the transcendent function. Through symbols, the transcendent, transformative function governs the process through which one thing changes into another. If you develop conscious awareness of its operation, it functions as your inner guiding principle and is a source of nourishment and healing.

The symbols of the transcendent function represent the union of different pairs of psychic opposites in a synthesis that transcends and reconciles them both. The uniting symbol only appears when you take your psychic life as seriously as you do daily life. It is just as valid, impacts you moment by moment, and carries psychological truth. This transcendent function restores the balance between the ego and the unconscious, sun and moon. It belongs to neither, yet possesses access to both. It lies in-between and, standing above it, participates in both. By relating to each mode independently, it unites ego and unconscious. This is known in Western mysticism as "cleansing the doors of perception"; in Eastern systems, it is called "access."

The inner guide takes the Son to the heights. This is analogous to the contemporary description of "peak experience" developed by Humanistic psychologist Abraham Maslow. Maslow has defined a peak experience as "a moment in the life of the individual when he felt strong, sure, and in complete control. He is fully functioning, and appears to an observer as more reliable, dependable, and trustworthy."

Masters and Houston (1966) elaborated on this description: "Specifically, the subject tends to feel that his encounter with Being has in some way led to the erasure of behavioral patterns blocking his development, and at the same time provides him with a new orientation complete with insight and energy sufficient to effect a dramatic and positive self-transformation."

Peak experiences reflect the upward mobility of the spirit in search of itself. These experiences are self-validating, self-justified, and have intrinsic value of a unique nature for each of us. You feel an intense experience of the nearness of your Higher Power. You may have had many spontaneous experiences of communing with nature, love in the fullest sense, feeling completely right about your life and who you are. In order to ground the insight and inspiration of these special moments, there is a psychosynthesis exercise for integrating transpersonal experiences. The content of this meditation reflects the holographic nature of this Lambsprinck plate.

There are two stages to the exercise. For the first phase, find a quiet, comfortable place and establish rhythmic breathing to relax your body and mind. When your mind becomes quiet, take time to recall a past transpersonal experience (like feeling at one with nature), filling in all the details with your mind so it is fully recreated in imagination. Relive the experience as vividly as you can by seeing, hearing, feeling, smelling, even tasting the scene. How much detail can you recall about your thoughts, feelings, and insights at the time? Where do you feel it in your body? Is it inside or outside? Notice any sensations, colors, impressions. When you "came back down" from the experience what new insights and understanding did you have? Did you try to share it? How did it change your life? Return to normal awareness and record your meditation in detail, especially its meaning.

Begin the second phase of the process in the same way, recalling the same experience you used in stage one. Focus on the most meaningful aspects, the central quality of the experience and summarize it with a symbol, a phrase, a word—whatever it means to you like serenity, joy, understanding, bliss. Next comes the step that echoes Lambsprinck's fourteenth-century vision: bring your imagination into the present and imagine the feeling you are standing at the top of a majestic mountain, the highest one around, on a crystal clear day. As you look toward the sun, you see a ray of light projecting toward you. From the sun a very Wise Old Man descends on the sunbeam, and you feel tremendous love emanating from him. Soon he arrives next to you on the summit.

You eagerly recount your transpersonal experience to this Wise One and ask what light he can shed on its meaning. Inquire about ways to integrate it into your life. Listen to his suggestions and seek clarification if you need it. Ask any sincere questions that come to mind. Take as long as you wish, but remember you may return anytime you like. Visualize yourself in the near future expressing the quality of your experience. How will you actualize it, in what specific circumstances? If obstacles arise, share them with the Wise Old Man and act on his suggestions. When you return to ordinary awareness, once again record what transpired.

See where in your work, life plans, and relationships you can begin expressing your new resource. Figure out how you want to do this and when. Stay realistic about your opportunities and limitations, and develop some small practical steps to implement the change into your present life. Resolve and affirm that you will express your new way of acting or being, making clear choices among various possibilities.

When the superconscious breaks through spontaneously, it is the result of profound inner processes. When you begin to integrate your transpersonal experiences, you ultimately leave behind the succession of peaks and valleys as you move toward a synthesis of the vertical (masculine/spiritual) and horizontal (feminine/soul) dimensions. If your Wise Old Man is critical or judgemental it is probably a subpersonality pretending to be your inner sage. Use your discrimination.

Another relevant psychosynthesis exercise is the dialogue with the Higher Self. It is based on the premise that man has a higher aspect, or soul, and that the personality can contact this higher aspect, seeking guidance. Everyone carries within a fount of wisdom, intuition, and a sense of purpose. The Self is the inner light of universal truth. It is your positive potential for more growth, strength, compassion, love, and wisdom than you could even imagine possible. Your inner wisdom source knows and understands you completely, both who you have been and your most meaningful future.

This exercise simply involves closing your eyes and tuning in to your own still center. Then you just imagine the face of your inner wisdom figure with eyes that express acceptance, love, and compassion for you. See eyes with the light of love, like God's eyes. Some people like to imagine the face appearing inside the opening bloom of a lotus or rose. Dialogue with this figure to your heart's content. Another alternative is to write a letter to your Higher Self, then switch roles and "answer" the letter as your inner wisdom figure. Soon the contact will be so strong that it will express itself as a kind of direct knowing of what the Higher Self is saying, even beyond images and words. You are incorporating—literally, "giving body to"—your wiser self into your daily self.

Use your common sense concerning information received. Is it really wise? Is it a vital step? Is it for the highest good? You may need to interpret the message even if you determine it is from the Higher Self. Examine any symbolic messages for their metaphorical resemblance to your concrete issues of the moment. The wisdom figure has a higher vantage point on your problems. But you still need to think them through mentally, as thoroughly as you can, before seeking this divine intervention. As your connection builds through frequent interchange, you feel your intrinsic worthiness and continue to align your will, mind, and emotions with your higher purpose.

A final exercise for this phase is to ask the Higher Self for understanding certain qualities or virtues better. Some that are enlightening to explore include Serenity, Harmony, Wisdom, Love, Joy, Compassion, Courage, Trust, and Surrender.

In terms of mystical meditation, this is the first state of grace or mind expansion. It is a response experience where you feel a sense of Presence. The true mystic takes this experience as his point of departure and grows in grace from it. The poet or artist bases artistic production on it, and also experiences personal euphoria. The higher perspective of the self is available and comes back into corporeal life through a myriad of images and metaphors including the circle, the ladder, the symbolic child, the butterfly, the ring, the star, the stone, the androgyne, etc. Experientially, it manifests as dreams, visions, synchronicity, sexual ecstasy (bliss and rapture), moments of clarity, and cosmic consciousness. Reflected on the four levels of awareness, the plate represents the following:

> *Spiritual Level*: The Soul is raised to the level of the Spiritual World, towards Union with God. But the process is not complete; it is imperfect if Matter is not identified with the Soul and Spirit. The Spirit therefore longs to return to Earth.
>
> *Mental Level*: Meditation, by which the mind is carried upward toward the plane of Ideas, may be begun with profit. The prerequisite is the conscious realization of the nature of your complexes and reintegration of your personality.
>
> *Emotional Level*: The emotions are transmuted through the purifying fires into a vision of the harmony of the universe. You have become more spontaneous, expressive, energetic, autonomous, confident, open, content, joyous, and self-accepting.

Physical Level: Contacting your inner guide through meditation indicates a withdrawal from the sensual aspects of the body to gain entry into the Spiritual World. You may become more ascetic, less hedonistic. Concentration requires the withdrawal of attention from the various sensory inputs. The plate also indicates the grounding of the transpersonal experience in applied wisdom.

After their ascent, the Son wishes to go back down to his Father, the body. The Guide agrees this is good for now. But he assures the prince that he will not let him go back down alone. The Guide will help the aspirant to ground the experience of the celestial heights. Spirit has been attracted back to the realm of Matter mainly through its attachment. Attachment is the downward pull on soul and spirit. Eastern yogis and Western ascetics have spoken volumes on attachment as a spiritual hindrance. Again, the metaphor of a continuing process of distillation is apt.

In alchemy, sublimation of the Spirit of a substance is caused by heating the gross Matter so the Spirit or Soul trapped in the medium becomes volatile and escapes upward. Then it returns to gross matter through condensation. The urge for transcendence, something greater than ourselves, pulls us up, and our attachments to body, spouse, ego, and the material realm pulls us down. The alchemical operation of this phase is *circulatio*, which unites the repetitive cycles of rising up and coming down. It means you circulate light around the aspects of your being. It is recycling of the *prima materia*. Sublimation ennobles your personality with the spiritual virtues. Coagulating means these insights and realizations begin to get integrated into your personality.

During this spiritual circulation your body becomes more sublime; in fact, you create a subtle body with the circulation of light. Spirit begins to manifest in your life in very concrete ways. By keeping the opposites in dynamic equilibrium you find new harmony. You learn to see through to the spirit hidden in matter. That which was formerly imaged as dead, is now suddenly seen as bursting with life. Sublimation is an alchemical form of resurrection, a revival and restoration of spiritual understanding. The increase in understanding is due to your expanded field of awareness. From the heights you gain a broad perspective. Grounding your peak experiences by writing them down and doing integration exercises helps materialize elusive intuitions and spiritual potential.

In the circulation spirit penetrates soul and soul envelops spirit. This is the basis of both the enactments of the eternal embrace in Tantra and sex magic. The participants are the cosmic lovers, identified with the divine qualities, oblivious to one another's personality level. He is spirit, She is soul. It is yang with a little yin embracing yin with a little yang that is the source of immortality. Swedenborg said "Sexual love is the purest energy of the divine state, for lovers in their embrace form one angel."

The High Peak of India is purported to lie in a vessel. That vessel may be imagined as the psyche, the hermetically sealed retort, or the cosmic Yoni. Whether the energy is called *Shakti, Shekinah, Sophia,* the Serpent Power, or *kundalini,* once it is awakened it has a powerful impact on all your systems. Meeting blockages, it creates symptoms of discomfort.

The way to move through this most quickly is to clear the blocks and circulate the energy. This serpent power is a basically sexual energy that is transmuted into spiritual potency as it ascends through the chakras. In this mutual embrace, there is a psychic revelation. The body becomes more subtle and the spirit gains body, or incarnates. Practically speaking, this means you are able to maintain your daily functionality without losing direct contact with the archetypal dimension.

Connectedness to daily life patterns is essential to balance your soul-travel in archetypal realms. This is easily done by maintaining ordinary pursuits except during an allotted meditation period. Marathon meditation is taboo at this point. Just circulate the light through your system during your chosen time, and practice consistently. Through your internal circulation, a spiritual earth or "mystical body" is created. And after all, matter in its subjective aspect is spirit, and spirit when regarded objectively is the material world. It is the world of limitation and repetitive cycles.

Circulation is an economic feedback-system that transforms your ego. Like the process of distillation, your essence is drawn out. This is an ecological recycling process done through the content of your experiences with archetypal patterns. This process of coordination is mediated by the *anima,* which is soul in the body. This will be the next step in Lambsprinck's process: getting the seemingly missing feminine aspect of soul back into the body. By continuing the process of circulation over time, you resurrect the soul of your body. You gain access to the knowledge of the soul through images as you circulate that light through every cell of your body.

What Jung called "coming to terms with the unconscious," the alchemists called meditation (*meditatio*). This was conceived and described as an internal dialogue with another who is invisible, as in the invocation of a Deity, or communion with one's self, or Angel. The alchemist willingly submits to the transpersonal totality of the psyche. This surrender allows room for grace to flow within. In short, we must empty ourselves to be filled.

Prior to establishing the connection with your Higher Self, you find your real self or deep center. It lies behind all of your self-images and self-concepts. It usually comes as a breakthrough experience, but one that is well grounded. It has to do with responsibility, honesty, and self-actualization. You no longer depend on defensiveness, projection, or rationalization. It brings a deep sense of self-respect and mind/body integration. At this stage you make the deep commitment to seek the mystical experience personally. You commit to and learn to trust your own experience, even if you accept outside spiritual direction. You take responsibility for whether or not you listen to your inner, directing voice.

Your soul naturally seeks knowledge of, and union with, an inner guiding principle. In the past, you may have found yourself spontaneously discussing aspects of your life with your source of inner wisdom, or perhaps an ancestor. Contacting your inner guide is merely a more conscious attempt at solidifying this relationship. In fact, throughout the Lambsprinck work, we have been in contact with this inner guiding principle, though it first appeared in animal forms. It takes a certain level of personality development to comprehend some of its aspects. As your consciousness develops, communication with the wisdom source and the reliability of the advice improves. Your ego interferes less with interpretations.

All of the preliminary mental training and integration of the personal aspects of the archetypes is designed to prepare you for meditation. Once you are able to meditate consistently and have a program for doing so, rituals of transformation are no longer necessary, but you may still enjoy their aesthetic quality. Your entire life is devoted and consecrated to the Great Work on a twenty-four hour-a-day basis.

If spiritual progress is your will, a living teacher with access to the highest mystical realms is the most efficient path to God-realization. But if you are not the student of a Master in a school of mystical meditation, you can still call on your inherent resources. This means dealing with your mind, and Universal Mind, through active imagination. You can meditate on contacting your inner Guru. After all, the outer Master always encourages the development of this inner form of the guru, guide, and friend.

This spiritual variant of contacting the inner guide begins with focusing your attention between the eyebrows, the so-called "third eye." Close your eyes and let impressions begin to guide your attention. Take an active role in the unfolding drama by using your subtle body. Preserve the feeling of looking out from your own eyes. Let each session be done with love and devotion. As you continue to knock, the door will surely open. With successive meditation periods, you may be given your Angel's name through intuition.

If this is the case, keep the name firmly in mind, repeating it while maintaining a sense of expectancy. Properly done, the Angel's countenance will appear spontaneously from the darkness, preceded by a faint glimmering of light and possibly some sounds like distant thunder or the roar of the surf. Once again, demand that any disembodied voice appear before you. Then, if it withstands testing, you may begin to ask questions.

True inner guides frequently appear in humanlike forms with ethereal wings or radiant auras. They always project a life-giving, healing, rejuvenating warmth, and produce feelings of absolute peace and serenity. Your inner guide probably won't speak spontaneously. You must question it directly, and you will only obtain answers if your ego is willing to truly accept the information. Again, don't spend too much time with frivolous questions about your love life, desires, the future, etc. The guide continues to function as your bridge to superconscious levels of awareness providing you don't succumb to ego interests.

Since mystical meditation is the best course left open for further soul growth, you might ask your Angel how to contact a living master who is qualified to initiate the soul on these levels. Contact with a living Saint is allegedly more efficient for the growth of a soul than contact with the inner guide (unless they have become synonymous). Nevertheless, ask your Angel, "How may I proceed further on my quest?" The Angel may offer suggestions, or its image may be replaced by the vision of your future teacher. This face may not be recognized until a much later time, when the Master is met on the physical plane. Continue to entreat the Angel about further progress and the answer will inevitably come forth. It is not even a matter of time, since the transcendent is a timeless/spaceless realm of actualized potential.

Remember, if you feel you have gotten a true contact with your Angel, you must apply its advice in your daily life in order to ground it. If you fail to use the advice practically, you may lose the contact and be unable to re-establish it. But, be sure you are tapping your higher mind, or you may be led irretrievably astray into a low level of psychism. Do not respond to a vague, psychic awareness of direction, but only to a face-to-face meeting on the inner planes, the divine nature of which is irrefutable. The experience must be dynamic enough for you to feel an irresistible impulse to fulfill your highest potential.

Usually inner guides are not going to volunteer any information at all, so be quite prepared to ask your questions during the overwhelming inspiration produced by the Angel. It could be helpful to formulate some questions beforehand, though you could revision them at any moment. If you enter active imagination at a lower plane, getting say an animal guide, be kind and gentle with it. It represents the instinctual side of the archetype and is your familiar or totem animal, your body wisdom.

Ask it who its superior is on the inner planes, and how to contact that being. Imagine you are rising on the planes of awareness and penetrating a higher level, and wait for that superior entity to contact you, as you focus on its name. When your attention is concentrated within, in a focused manner, archetypal forces are awakened and revealed to you. Awareness of daily life, its problems and sensory impulses, is suspended during the meditation for contacting your Angel.

Upon completion of your session, be sure to record any results in your diary or journal. If the contact is poorly defined, watch your dreams for the next few days for further insight, or suggestions. If these seem consistent with your spiritual values, work with these suggestions in your next meditation period.

Caution: Never attempt any work on the inner planes with the use of intoxicants. Psychedelics may seem to free your imagination, but they also cloud your mind, and inhibit your higher faculties of discrimination. They may produce a seeming mind-expansion, but it is merely a trick of the mind, a "creative regression" to amniotic bliss. The experience may subjectively feel spiritual and, to some extent, may be an experience of universal wholeness. However, it is different for everyone, every time, and is never repeatable at will.

You should be able to use imagination and meditation to enter these regions and withdraw from them at will; don't allow yourself to be merely swept away into the phantasmagoria of the Universal Mind. Your mental faculties need to be fully present, not diminished or overwhelmed. Alchemy is not a shamanistic pursuit. When you enter "holy ground" the mind should be cleansed and pure. Then you will be much more able to integrate your experience constructively.

This creative Archetypal Imagination is another refinement of simple Active Imagination. It is designed for an experience of the higher mind, through which you can perceive the pure form of the archetypes as they appear in your mind. At this level, they are not contaminated by your personal complexes. They are more themselves, and less colored by your personal bias, or expectations. Your spirit guide may be a high archetype. At first it appears to be outside of you, but taking it seriously you get closer over time. You eagerly fulfill its requirements, and ultimately become identified with it.

This is essentially a polytheistic phase, where you acknowledge the existence of many spiritual beings, though you prefer certain ones. Over time you realize this higher being is a projection of your superconscious and make a personal breakthrough. You now perceive your own sacred nature and re-own your holiness, or wholeness. You project the higher Self, as the Self projects you. Instead of being circumspect, you realize what it is to be "synchro-spect."

By personifying the Higher Self (as Angel, guide, or Guru), we can develop feelings of loving devotion that open the heart. This opening shifts emphasis from a mental mode to one that is spontaneously uplifting. The Angel is a personified soul-image in the tradition of the alchemical *anima mundi* or the Eastern Gurus and Sat Gurus (Saints or Masters). It is the inspiring *daimon* or muse in its most exalted form.

Do not be overly concerned about the sex of your inner guide. There is no basis for gender identification at this level. The guide can appear in many forms. Most often the inner Self of a man is male, while the inner most aspect of a woman is female. The being most frequently appears to be androgynous or asexual, since it represents paradoxical wholeness. A woman initiated by a male Master will experience the higher Self in this form without hampering her connection to the divine Feminine.

A female teacher for a man enhances his ability to perceive his soul in female form, as *anima*. Hence, we hear teachers like Sri Aurobindo speaking of "the Mother." The main point is to follow the path of meditation outlined by your spiritual guide. In the text, the peak of India refers to Mt. Meru, symbol of successive stages of ascent of the soul through meditation. This line shows that the reference is to mystical meditation, which is traditionally, even characteristically, associated with India.

You are now not far from your goal. You have healed your shadow/persona split and discovered your own dark side; you are learning to harmonize masculine and feminine energies; you have journeyed to your spiritual heights and primitive depths. You have overcome many spiritual hindrances like arrogance. You have brought a torch of consciousness into your unconscious and owned your share of divinity. The crises created enough chaos to breakdown obstacles to further development.

The Self provided both inner and outer impetus for your journey to self-realization. You have found the psychic midpoint. You are a well-rounded individual. You are becoming a Self by widening your ego with knowledge of the unconscious. You can reflect on how your experiment has changed your values, aims, and actions in the world.

The experience of the Self is a continuing encounter with your inner god-image. You see it, and you see it seeing you. Your ego feels like it is under the scrutiny of the Eye of God, and this is the ordeal of this phase of transformation. Becoming conscious requires this seeing and being seen, knowing and being known. This is the essence of the I-Thou relationship. There is a reciprocal effect on ego-consciousness and Self-consciousness. The personality becomes aware of the transpersonal center and begins living that awareness, creating an incarnation of the divine. The call of the Self enlisted the ego long ago. Can you recall what experiences led you into the Great Work?

God is carried experientially by individuals ethical enough to choose the Good; then the incarnation is psychic experience. So the god-image in the psyche is virtually indistinguishable from God. And this God-image in the psyche is the Self. Creative contact with this inward transforming experience is stabilized. The coming to terms with the archetypal world is done largely through the mediation of the inner Friend, Guide, Guardian, or Angel, who is the archetype of The Way.

The Guide helps you hold the delicate balance of opposites, the deep center. There is an influx of energy, wisdom, strength, and tremendous creativity. The Self is the very source of love, and this is ultimately the energy of integration. Your core-self is your deep center and the seed of your being. This creativity helps you stand up to the problems of physical life. The creative contact can be brought into the outer world, brought back down into the body, into corporeality, made to matter. The inward transformation is still the primary experience.

The visionary journey with your psychic companion leads you to internalize the whole cosmos and changes you into a seer. The healthy ego sacrifices itself on the altar of wholeness. You see through the worldly illusion of *maya*. Every sorrow has taken you another step on the Path. You make peace with death. The inner companion is there to offer solace and comfort. It pulls you into blissful states. You notice the purposeful energy of your psyche as an autonomous force. The relationship with this symbol makes it possible to experience a mystery that cannot be touched, and you just surrender to those depths.

"The Father swallows up the Son"

PLATE 13

"Son, in your absence I was dead,
And my life was great misery;

But now you are here I am alive again,
And your return gives me great joy."

But when the Son enters his Father's house,
The Father takes him in his arms,
And swallows him up in that same hour,
Devouring him with his own mouth.
The great exertion makes the Father sweat.

The Father swallows up the Son.

Soul, Spirit, and Matter are made one.

Chapter 13: Devouring Father

Conception

IN this passage Matter says that he was dead, because physical life contains an immortal, transpersonal quality only when it is purposefully linked with the Spirit. Humanity, without a spiritual component, is hardly better off than the animals. Alchemically, the plate illustrates the third process of Distillation. Having risen to the top of the vessel, the distillate, or essence, precipitates back down into Matter. This entry, or re-entry, of Spirit into Matter, is analogous to *conception*—the life force becomes corporeal. Matter willingly consumes Spirit. Deity becomes substance.

Once again, we may examine just what this distillation process signifies on the four major levels of experience:

> *Spiritual Level*: The Spirit is absorbed by Matter.
>
> *Mental Level*: After meditation the mind returns to dwelling on mundane affairs.
>
> *Emotional Level*: After the exaltation of emotions, or mystic ecstasy, the normal emotional level is resumed and refocused on mundane objects.
>
> *Physical Level*: Matter is given life and consciousness by its association with Spirit. Without its spiritual component, matter may as well be "dead." Its impact tends to disperse the gross matter's tendency to inertia, allowing Matter to "evolve."

The illustration reiterates that the son is Spirit and the father is Body. The father must devour the son in order that the Soul and Spirit may be freed from the Body later for rebirth (see next plate). The spiritual principle of Light and Logos sinks into the embrace of physical nature. In alchemy the son and the sun are synonymous.

An infusion of light ("seeing god") and the power of the audible life stream ("hearing God") enters the body during a session of meditation. The rejuvenating effect is felt in the body as a kind of "afterglow," *joie de vivre*. The body did, in fact, feel deserted and abandoned during the flight of Spirit and Soul because all the consciousness was drawn up and away from the physical senses and concentrated at the eye center. Sensory input was severely restricted. Still, the downward pull of the body is a constant hindrance in meditation. Even after stilling the mind, and communing with God and the angels, you can be drawn back quickly by an itch, an ache, or outside intrusion.

Meditation is a "tuning up" procedure practiced on the path of transcendence. It functions as a means of cleaning the mind, much like therapy clears the personal subconscious. Meditation reorients the mind, and saints say it burns off karma. Some of the benefits of meditation, like centering, grounding, stress management, insight, and detachment, can be gained through the will and discipline of the ego alone. Paradoxically, however, meditation is a procedure used to gain independence from the ego. Any benefits of meditation that aid outer adaptation to life can be considered to feed the process of self-actualization. If they aid inner development, they feed self-realization.

The mystical components of meditation like contact bliss, rapture, and knowledge states, are the results of grace alone. The individual reaches inwardly toward the Self, patiently receptive to the influx of the Self. Hindering thoughts cease. The body becomes intimately involved in the transformation process. The superconscious infusion may not be perceived as "spiritual" energy if you do not meditate. Spontaneous manifestations include altruism, service to others, new concepts, insights or values.

You meditate seeking direct experience of your Higher Self nature for a direct experience of the Higher Self is undeniably spiritual. The Self is usually very insistent about changes it would like to see you implement. Meditation facilitates this process of allowing the superconscious to emerge from within. Meditation is a time to experience just being and not resisting an influx of transpersonal energy. In this way you expose yourself to integratable experience, opening yourself to subtle transformation. You learn to identify with the higher structure of reality and to perceive reality from the higher perspective of Deity.

Instead of thinking about the superconscious in concepts at the mental level, you experience its transformative power through subtle forms in the spiritual realm. You experience contact, not just visions. You surrender to the inflowing grace without avoidance, for total acceptance is safe and natural. At this stage, you are touched by God. This is the psychedelic or consciousness-expanding phase. It is mind manifesting. "Descent of the force" is one of the first signs of enlightenment.

With enough grace, you move beyond subject-object dualism into unity. And then you come back to the body, back to body/world awareness, and discover your transcendence is not from the world, but *into* the world. You now operate from your identification with Deity whenever possible. The object is to make the realization constant in the waking state. You personally realize Deity as creator and sustainer of all life and being. This mystic ecstasy means once again giving up your old identity and changing through death/rebirth.

This state is another great leap forward, another quantum leap into the oceanic experience of cosmic consciousness, and a leap into the yawning mouth of Matter. Death in this case represents the completion of the spirit's descent into matter, sort of an ultimate coagulation. It is as if we, as humans, are really dead, unless we are awakened to our higher faculties of the Spirit. In touch with the Self, you proclaim "Now that you are here, I am alive again." This is a conjunction, a joining of two principles. So long as consciousness refrains from acting, the opposites remain dormant in the unconscious and the Self does not constellate, and grace is nowhere to be found.

Once the higher faculties have been activated, the son or Spirit is swallowed up. This means that the body and the psychic representatives of the organs gain mastery over the conscious mind. An analogy of this occurs in the process of meditation when your attention is diverted from concentration by the body—that persistent itch, or rumbling in the intestines, or a cramp, etc. In the hero myths this state is depicted as being swallowed by a whale or a dragon. The resulting heat of the digestive process is usually quite intense. Thus we see in the next plate that, after swallowing the son, the father "sweats" a lot.

The prototype image of "devouring father" is the myth of Saturn eating his children. Father Time ultimately claims all at death, devouring all forms or patterns. Psychologically, the archetypal father-image is paradoxical. At one pole, as guardian of his children, he protects them from outside threats. On the other hand, the father devours the children and their spontaneity with his rigid feelings, behavior, and insistence on conventional thought and behavior. Physically, the body functions as the carrier of consciousness and preserves its integrity. However, the body is habituated to certain behaviors that make spiritual realization nearly impossible.

A reflection of this negative father image is seen in people whose consciousness is tied, bound, and swallowed up in conventional thoughts and habits. This may be fine socially, but it is spiritual suicide. If your spirituality is swallowed in conventionality you can never reach your individual potential. This was a major issue during Lambsprinck's time. The nature and effect of the Holy Ghost became a big controversy in the Church in the Middle Ages. Christ said God would send the Comforter, and he intimated that those who received this spirit would be able to do works even greater than his.

The Holy Ghost descends upon people and fills them directly with the spirit of God, continuing the incarnation of God. This implies that if you are filled with the Holy Ghost you can understand the Holy Scriptures directly and symbolically, rejecting the interpretations of the Church. This eventually led to the Reformation, which alleged that each individual has the right to communicate with God directly. And this, of course, is the mystic quest.

In terms of your spiritual process, this means you are not necessarily "wrong" to determine your duties and responsibilities by prevailing collective norms, but it may limit your spiritual potential. Society, as a collective, tends to favor the lowest common denominator. It is simply a matter of priorities. How much priority, especially time-wise, do you allot for spiritual practice? Just showing up for church on Sunday and doing a few good works may not satisfy the "inner Master." Our society is riddled with the degeneration of cultural values, tastes, and opinions. If you unquestioningly adopt life patterns from your cultural milieu, it may erode your individual capacity for spontaneous reaction.

You can still "fit in" with society and maintain your unique individual spiritual quest, if you remember the dictum to "render unto Caesar" *and* God/dess. This represents the harmonizing of your physical and spiritual aspects since it provides a means for both to flourish. This is the idea behind spending a portion of each day in meditation practice. You come alive to your own values and morals through your individual conscience, rather than accepting the censoring authority of some outside agent.

The biased values of those who currently dominate society are sometimes "shoved down our throats." There is trouble when consensus opinion takes the place of informed opinion born of personal experience. Deep meaning is the essence of your existence as a physical being, and this comes only through personal experience of the spiritual dimension of life.

The Great Work does not demand that you "fly up" to the heavens and abandon your responsibilities on earth. To the contrary, it is a householder's path, which requires only consistent and diligent effort on a daily basis. It is best to set aside a prescribed amount of time daily allotted to inner work. Then stick to your program of meditation and self-discovery. This is a positive means of dealing with the devouring aspects of social or collective life. It is a mature response that meets the needs both of upward spiritual mobility and the downward pull of physicality. Alchemy is a solitary work. At this stage it has to do with digesting your reclaimed spiritual projections.

Identifying too heavily with either your spirituality or physicality can lead to a negative response. A counterfeit spirituality can manifest as obsessive anti-authoritarianism, or anarchism. A better solution is autarchy, or self-rule, not lawlessness. Even the deliberate eccentric or systematic nonconformist are reacting collectively, not as true individuals. The reactionary stance is still in conflict, dualistic, or polarized. And this reaction polarizes the opposites within rather than harmonizing them. The renegade or maverick finds it impossible to realize his true individuality. It's as though his negative father complex has him in its mouth, grinding away with its accusations of unmet expectations. Just imagine a captain-of-industry type of father, and a son who would like to become a monk, or an alternative-type healer, or even a poet.

Culture only provides a narrow pathway for advancing into a secure niche in the status quo. It also makes sure that any alternative is considered "selfish" at the least and complete failure or annihilation at worst. The devouring father within presses your consciousness toward more conventional behavior patterns. This split between conscious and unconscious maintains the ruling, dominant attitudes of your culture. This is done by depriving your consciousness of instinctual or irrational reactions. Thus, through cancelling the possibility of revolutionary change or transformation, a creative future can be aborted.

This is a juncture in the life of many individuals when they seek "right livelihood." It may become a real issue at midlife when inner life demands a change from a "job" to a vocation or career more in harmony with ethical and spiritual principles. It would be difficult to carry on, for example, as a high-pressure salesperson who is required by employers to lie and cheat customers. The ethical dilemma is impossible to carry, so one seeks work where God-given talents can be used and true service offered.

In the plate, we also see the presence of the Guide, standing there as if conducting the entire scenario. His right hand is up symbolizing spirit; the left hand is down symbolizing matter. The Guide is the alchemical Spirit *Mercurius*, also known as Hermes the Mystagogue. It is the archetype of the unconscious and the process of individuation. Various authors attribute it to both spirit and soul, and in this instance it stands as the uniting factor of both. The ambiguity reflects a characteristic quality of the psyche.

According to alchemical writings, *Mercurius* is a transformative substance that unites all conceivable opposites. The dualistic nature of Mercurius is revealed through androgyny, materiality, and spirituality. *Mercurius* is a psychic phenomenon that transcends the spirit-body dilemma. It is described as both fiery and watery, and the baptisms of fire and water in Lambsprinck reflect this aspect. Another dual aspect is *senex/puer*.

The hermaphroditic nature of *Mercurius* begins emerging in this plate and continues in the next. The dead masculine body becomes softer and more feminine and opens to the entrance of the spirit. This feminized body opens itself to penetration by the spirit and conceives by virtue of the Holy Ghost. The sickness and purgation that ensue are a necessary part of the conditions for rebirth in which the Self acts as the central, guiding principle.

The archetype of *Mercurius*, or Hermes, can be traced back to Egypt where he was known as Thoth, Lord of Magic. In Greece, Hermes was messenger of the gods, mediating between heaven and earth. Alchemical tracts speak of *Mercurius* ascending from earth to heaven and descending again to earth, receiving the powers of Above and Below. This sequence ends when he returns to earth with complete power.

As alchemist or mystic you start from below, ascend on high, and with the powers of Above and Below united in yourself, you return to earth again. You express the circular nature of *Mercurius* when you circulate the light. *Mercurius* is an arcane substance which the text depicts as an alchemical Trinity, to clarify its correspondence with God.

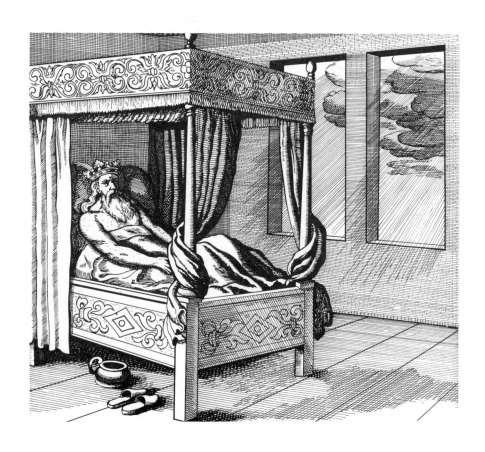

"The Father strongly sweats and glows"

182

PLATE 14

The Father sweats, surrounding his Son,
And pours out his prayer to God,
To Whom all things are possible,
Who creates, and has created all things.

He prays that his Son may be led from his body,
And be reborn as he was at first.

God grants his prayer, it is not ignored,
Telling the Father to lie down and go to sleep.

God sent down rain from heaven
Through the clear stars; in truth,
It was fruitful silver indeed.

The Father's body is moistened and softened.
By the help and grace of God, at the end,
We may obtain thy gracious Gift!

The Father strongly sweats and glows,
While oil and the True Tincture from him flows.

"The Father strongly sweats and glows."

Chapter 14: Anima Consciousness

Incubation

E ATING the son seems to have made the father ill so he has taken to his bed. Another example of the archetype of the sick king appears in the legends of the Grail King. The sick king is the one who was born perfect but now suffers from spiritual sterility. He may only be healed or brought back to life by the *elixir vitae*, the liquid aspect of the Stone. To the impure, the tincture or divine water is a deadly poison; for those who come through the purgation, it cures and ennobles. What is needed is a return of the missing, rejected Feminine through moistening and softening. Thus, a baptism with water follows the baptism by fire of the feverish state.

Lacking psychological insight, a person might have this myth play through life involuntarily and unconsciously. It can still have a profound transformative effect. Consider, for example, a workaholic executive. He may entirely repress his feeling nature and spirituality in favor of the cultural dream of material success. But then suddenly something happens—a heart attack lays him low. In the grip of his malady new revelations may appear. He may suddenly recognize the value of loved ones and nearness to God from his hospital bed. Now he has the time to attend consciously to these matters while business and material concerns fade into the background.

Confronted by a brush with death, he sweats, fever or not. He sweats out the disposition of his spiritual nature, weighing his life in the balance. The sickness enforces the formerly repressed introversion and reflection. If he survives he may indeed be reborn into an entirely new lifestyle. He is baptized by the Holy Spirit, which may heal him. If it takes, he may develop a more well-rounded, holistic perspective on life. Others, once recovered, may slide back into materialistic philosophy. After initial prayers for grace are answered, they may revert to old habit patterns. Thus, the next heart attack. The lucky ones develop an open heart, healing themselves and perhaps others, as well. The concreteness of literal open-heart surgery becomes transformed into a spiritual state of an open heart and expanded mind.

A mystic confronts this stage much more consciously. All aspects of this profound transformation are covered by Christian mystic St. John of the Cross in his spiritual classic, *The Dark Night of the Soul*. The dark night is a period of purgative contemplation wherein a soul that has known a high degree of spiritual intimacy experiences a subjective negation of itself, its spirituality, and all things. One is no longer a beginner, but proficient when God seemingly withdraws spiritual favors. Prior, the soul found joy in lengthy periods of prayer, but now meditation is dry and fruitless, becoming virtually impossible. The comforter who shared consolation and spiritual grace so freely is nowhere to be found.

The passive purgation of the dark night is actually a more subtle grace. You cannot actively purify yourself enough to merit union, but God sends the divine cure in the form of a dark fire, or "fever." It is emotional and spiritual "burnout." You feel "burnt out." The dark night strengthens and purifies your love of God, but before it does so it makes you lose sight of it.

St. John says one reason is that we seek the delight and satisfaction of religious practices; in other words, we seek more than spiritual purity or discretion. Through pure *dryness* and interior darkness we are weaned from spiritual gratifications and delights. Mystics call this phase of meditation "licking the dry stone." Even the ecstasies of the initial stages are felt only because your sensory channels are overwhelmed.

The dark night cleanses both the sensory and spiritual aspects of the soul. The sensory purgation was illustrated in the last Plate, when the body experienced itself as if it were dead. The senses are purged and "accommodated to the spirit." In the spiritual purgation, the soul is denuded and prepared for union with God through love. The sensory night is a fairly common experience; but the spiritual night comes only to the proficient. Still, it is horrible and frightful to the spirit, for God darkens all the light, and closes the way to the spring of sweet spiritual water the aspirant was tasting as often and as long as desired.

These souls are inconsolable, finding no sweetness or delight in anything. Furthermore, their new distaste for things spiritual causes them to think they have turned their backs on God. These aridities purge the sensory appetite and produce an inclination for solitude and quiet. The imperfect state is like the sleeping state from which the mystic is awakened as from death to a new life by the divine tincture. God has given a way for freeing ourselves from the natural, imperfect sleeping state by bathing in the higher state of enlightenment or higher consciousness, which ennobles base substances. It takes a while to tune in to the savor of this inner balm, since it is so delicate.

Actually, God is speaking to the soul through pure spirit in the act of simple contemplation where there is no thought. You are powerless to meditate, deprived of both sensory and spiritual satisfaction. Your soul feels it has gone astray and been abandoned by God. The soul should rest in quiet contemplation with patience and persevere in prayer. God is liberating the soul from its constraints with the mind.

St. John recommends that "They must be content simply with a loving and peaceful attentiveness to God, and live without the concern, without the effort, and without the desire to taste or feel Him," since this distracts the soul from its infused blessing. This contemplation is "nothing else than a secret and peaceful and loving inflow of God, which, if not hampered, fires the soul in the spirit of love." It kindles divine love.

For each step toward Union there is an ordeal. This one is the "sickness unto death." St. John likens it to undergoing a cure which is the suffering of a dark and dry purgation of the appetites, a purification of the soul. The soul is freed from vice by quenching its earthy and spiritual craving. The soul enters the second dark night on pure faith, having learned knowledge of self and personal misery. It now recognizes its truly humble reality, and feels its powerlessness to serve God better. God illuminates the darkness by also showing the soul his grandeur and majesty, when that soul is open to wisdom, empty and unhindered. Spiritual humility comes from being purged of the vice of pride that develops when you feel like God's chosen.

When the appetites have withered, you live in spiritual sobriety, peace, and tranquility. The soul resides in habitual remembrance of God; it is purged of anger, envy, and sloth. Lambsprinck echoes the words of St. John: "Softened and humbled by aridities and hardship and by other temptations and trials in which God exercises the soul in the course of this night, a person becomes meek toward God and himself, and also toward his neighbor."

This comes to one who has "calmed the four passions (joy, sorrow, hope and fear) through constant mortification, and lulled to sleep the natural sensory appetites. . . .When this house of the senses is stilled (that is, mortified), its passions quenched, and its appetites calmed and put to sleep through this happy night of the purgation of the senses, the soul went out in order to begin its journey along the road of the spirit." This is the Illuminative Way of infused contemplation. God himself then refreshes the soul.

The purified sensory part of the soul begins experiencing the delights of the spirit, without the load of the corruptible body on the soul. When the process is perfected, ecstasies, raptures and bodily torments cease, "and they enjoy freedom of spirit without a detriment to or transport of their senses." There is no more affect overload, but full consciousness of the influx of divine energy. In the first purgation the senses become accommodated to the spirit; for the union with the spirit of God, the stains of the "old man" must be further purged. The spirit becomes attentive, illumined, and clarified.

The spiritual purgation includes seductive fantasies, vain visions, and false prophecies. The mind comes disguised as god or saints, and seeks to trap the soul in the creation. The senses aren't even really purged until the second phase; the first just bridles them. St. John says this is because, "all the imperfections and disorders of the sensory part are rooted in the spirit and from it receive their strength. All good and evil habits reside in the spirit and until these habits are purged, the senses cannot be completely purified of their rebellions and vices."

He continues:

> Wishing to strip them in fact of this old man and clothe them with the new, which is created according to God in the newness of sense, God divests the faculties, affections, and senses, both spiritual and sensory, interior and exterior. He leaves the intellect in darkness, the will in aridity, the memory in emptiness, and the affections in supreme affliction, bitterness, and anguish, by depriving the soul of the feeling and satisfaction it previously obtained from spiritual blessings.

Purgation allows the soul to stand naked before God. St. John's comment on this is worth considering verbatim. He expresses it in the words of the soul itself:

> Poor, abandoned, and unsupported by any of the apprehensions of my soul (in the darkness of my intellect, the distress of my will, and in the affliction and anguish of my memory), left to darkness in pure faith, which is a dark night for these natural faculties, and with only my will touched by the sorrows, affliction, and longings of love of God, I went out from myself. That is, I departed from my low manner of understanding, and my feeble way of loving, and my poor and limited method of finding satisfaction in God. I did this unhindered by either the flesh or the devil.
>
> This was a great happiness and a sheer grace for me, because through the annihilation and calming of my faculties, passions, appetites and affections, by which my experience and satisfaction in God was base, I went out from my human operations and way of acting to God's operation and way of acting. That is:
>
> My intellect departed from itself, changing from human and natural

to divine. For, united with God through this purgation, it no longer understands by means of its natural vigor and light, but by means of the divine wisdom to which it was united.

And my will departed from itself and became divine. United with the divine love, it no longer loves in a lowly manner, with its natural strength, but with the strength and purity of the Holy Spirit; and thus the will does not operate humanly in relation to God.

And the memory, too, was changed into presentiments of eternal glory.

He thus concludes, "finally, all the strength and affections of the soul by means of this night and purgation of the old man, are renewed with divine qualities and delights."

The purgation brings affliction and torment only because the wisdom of the divine exceeds the capacity of the soul. The more impure the soul, the more pain. The great divine light of contemplation casts a spiritual darkness over the soul only because it shines in a dark, impure soul. St. John says:

Since this divine contemplation assails him somewhat forcibly in order to subdue and strengthens his soul, he suffers so much in his weakness that he almost dies, particularly when the light is more powerful. Both the senses and the spirit, as though under an immense and dark load, undergo such agony and pain that the soul would consider death a relief. Since the divine extreme strikes in order to renew the soul and divinize it (by stripping it of habitual affections and properties of the old man to which it is strongly united, attached, and conformed), it so disentangles and dissolves the spiritual substance—absorbing it in a profound darkness—that the soul at the sight of its miseries feels that it is melting away and being undone by a cruel spiritual death; it feels as if it were swallowed by a beast and being digested in the dark belly, and it suffers an anguish comparable to Jonah's when in the belly of the whale. It is fitting that the soul be in this sepulcher of dark death in order that it attain the spiritual resurrection for which it hopes.

The purgative contemplation is oppression in the valley of the shadow of death. You painfully feel God's absence, a sense of rejection and unworthiness, and it seems to go on forever. Your temporal, natural and spiritual resources have dried up, and you feel your imperfection acutely; you are in darkness and abandoned by spirit. This creates a sacred emptiness, a sacred void. It is purified when God purges both the sensory and spiritual substance of your soul. St. John writes that "the sensory part is purified by aridity, the faculties by the void of their apprehensions, and the spirit by thick darkness."

The great endarkening comes before the great enlightening. All your attachments and imperfect habits accumulated over a lifetime are rooted deeply in the substance of the soul. They are uprooted in the service of spiritual emptiness. In fact, "the affliction suffered in the emptiness and poverty of both the sensory and the spiritual substance of the soul" is the Void or the Abyss.

God only humbles the soul to exalt it afterwards, but the exaltations are still emergent. St. John explains, "If he did not ordain that these feelings, when quickened in the soul, be soon *put to sleep* again, a person would die in a few days. Only at intervals is one aware of these feelings in all their intensity." There is no remedy from spiritual council or doctrine "until his spirit is humbled, softened, and purified, until it becomes so delicate, simple, and refined that it can be one with the Spirit of God, according to the degree of union of love that God in His mercy, desires to grant."

To be really effective, the purgation usually has to last for years with alternating cycles of purification and loving illumination, with an abundance of spiritual communication. When the communion is strong, we lose sight of our impurities, but feel something remains to be done. St. John remarked that, "It feels as though an enemy is within it who, although pacified and *put to sleep*, will awaken and cause trouble." So, when you feel safest, another round comes to engulf you, even more dark and severe than the last. But this night both darkens the spirit and gives it light.

Without purgation, the soul could not experience such an abundance of spiritual delight. Darkness only lasts long enough to annihilate your intellect's habitual way of understanding and let divine light take its place. "The darkness seems to be substantial darkness, since it is felt in the deep substance of the spirit." Alternately, the serenity that comes with the communication of mystical knowledge is ineffable. This only happens when the lower operations, passions, and appetites of the soul are *put to sleep* or quelled by this night.

All your faculties must be passive and purified to receive this infusion of grace. It is God's grace that all the passions, affections, and appetites which live in your sensory and spiritual parts are *put to sleep*, mortified, deadened, depriving you of the ability to find pleasure in anything. Even your imagination is impeded. All faculties become empty and useless, and this makes way for that emptiness to become infused with divinity.

The symbols of dark water and clouds hide a soul from divinity when it comes close to God's dwelling place. *The Cloud of Unknowing* is a classic mystical text. Here, we find silver rain changing to clear water in the next stanza of Lambsprinck's process. The Holy Spirit infuses communication on the soul; like a bridegroom it enters the bridal chamber. The experience is ineffable.

Returning to the alchemical metaphor, we find in this plate that the gross matter has become identified with Spirit; by the application of fire (fever), it gives off a vapor which rises and becomes volatile. On reaching the top of the retort this vapor cools and condenses (aspirations fade), falling back onto gross matter.

At each circulation the Body becomes more closely identified with the Spirit and vice versa. We may examine this distillation process on four levels of reality:

> *Spiritual Level:* This is the Dark Night of the Soul. The process of alternate cycles of aspiration toward the Spiritual world and involvement in the world of Matter through the physical body continues.
>
> *Mental Level:* Repetition of the cycle at the mental level. The mind is purged either through meditation and contemplation which reorients attitudes, or by the various experiences of life, which tend to force a change of attitudes by increasing environmental difficulties when the attitude is incorrect. In this way mental blockages are destroyed.
>
> *Emotional Level:* Purging through devotion to the Great Work, or the sublimation of passionate and elemental forces into Love, will result in detachment and freedom from the unbalanced emotional and subconscious ties resulting from karma or incorrect attitudes.
>
> *Physical Level:* The body evolves towards perfection and changes in the course of its interaction with the Spirit, giving off sweat or effete matter. "Glowing" is probably a reference to the radiant haloes so frequently pictured around the heads of saints and sages.

The keyword here is sacrifice: sacrifice of the old self for the new Self. It is a further seeking for the point of equilibrium. We are crucified in the flesh on the Cross of the elements. We are born into the discipline of the world of matter. But we may sacrifice this and appeal for grace from on high. God responds to Lambsprinck's entreaties. When your soul is "sick unto death" you must sacrifice your material concerns for a time each day for meditation and contemplation. When you "die daily" you gain access to God's grace, the life-giving moisture, the tincture.

This healing balm is called *amrita*, or spiritual nectar, in India. It appears as the food or drink of the gods in the Vedic myths, some of the oldest known holy scriptures. *Amrita* is the nectar of immortality, a cleansing spiritual dew. In the Vedic text it is identified with the *soma* drink. And Soma is also a deity that is a personification of the moon. This nectar is the mother's milk for the reborn sage. It flows from the celestial Goddess, in contrast to the mothering Earth Goddess. This draught infuses new vigor and in myth gave Vishnu the ability to defeat demons. This sacred juice is the luminous distillation of heaven. There is allegedly an analog created in the brain as a secretion of the pineal body. It is the sweet water of life.

The nature of water is to always be receptive and seek its own level. It is reflective and quiescent when still. Water cleanses by flowing through and flooding, moistening, softening, melting. This spiritual water soothes the burnt out emotions. It corresponds to the emotional or feeling aspect of experience. When your cup overflows with the water of life you feel abundance. It is appropriate that water appears in this phase of gestation and rebirth, for it echoes the development of a fetus in amniotic fluid. As this nectar floods through the psyche it opens blocked channels.

Water can also symbolize Deity as process, a feminine aspect of celestial divinity. Rain comes down from above. Celestial rain is a transpersonal blessing. Deity is not approached as subject or object (Thou), but as process. It is not yet pure energy, but is finer than Deity as substance (Many in One). You experience it as Otherness and Oneness by entering into it and being it, and emerging from it enriched. It is more than Spirit, Love, or True Will. This stage is best accomplished with commitment, worship, and the company of other believers. This is not total unity since love still implies two.

It is the paradox of Other/One, which even transforms the good/evil polarity here. At this level, evil becomes fully taken up into the self-movement of Deity itself, and the contradiction is solved. You simply make your will good. Just watch your choices concerning belief systems. You will have many theological questions now. You need a mental concept for external understanding, which you can give up later. At each stage what you have to understand becomes more difficult, and at each stage giving up your old paradigm becomes harder.

Another paradox embodied in this plate is the inner experience of "the Void" and "the Plenum." They are paradoxical opposites, one being sacred emptiness and the other divine fullness. This text seems to indicate an alternation in the distillation process between these extremes. On the one hand, we have spiritual practitioners and mystics like St. John of the Cross,

Zen monks, and Tibetan Buddhists extolling the virtues of the imageless void. On the other, the correspondences of water, rain, nectar of immortality, silver and the moon suggest a relation to the super-celestial *Anima* as the hidden, secret, or concealed feminine element which rounds out the Trinity of Father, Son, and Holy Spirit. Feminine, diffuse consciousness suggests a "fullness" rather than emptiness. *Anima* is always linked to soul. Psychology speaks for the soul in an interestingly different way than pure Logos, or spirit.

In this plate, the feverish father sweats the tincture of the wise from his body. The hidden fire causing the sweat is the antithesis of the moisture it produces. This heat is the warmth of incubation, which is equivalent to a "brooding" state of meditation. The aim of this meditation is the same as the yogic exercise *tapas*, which is self-incubation for transformation and resurrection.

When Ignatius Loyola recommended imagination through the five senses, he was aiming for the fullest possible realization of the object of contemplation. This increases your capacity to concentrate and obtain clarity of thought. In contrast, the alchemist projects himself into the realm of soul-making or "*anima*-ted" consciousness. In this state the ego does not see itself as it would like, free of all blemishes and shortcomings. Rather, it sees itself objectively.

During this stark look at itself, darkness represses the spirit. All the psychic happenings are down in the feminine depths. Something is gestating within, feasting on the nectar of spiritual immortality. The repression producing the illness is healed by reintroduction of the feminine aspect of celestial divinity. This is symbolized by the moon, moisture, and silver. It is a softening process that produces flow—balance between solar and lunar types of consciousness. Spirit corresponds with the sun and is linear, analytical, and goal oriented. Moon is soulful, diffuse, synthetic, and process oriented. Solar brilliance and moon madness are classically distinct, but they may be conjoined, or married to one another. James Hillman, Jungian analyst, characterized this form of wholeness as "illumined lunacy." This is one of the attributes used to describe many saints and mystics throughout history.

Silver indicates cleansing and purifying, or becoming more essential and durable. It also represents the full moon's brightness, its completion or elevation. This is an image of full-term pregnancy, which necessarily precedes rebirth. The king becomes feminized through his illness before he can give rebirth. He must become reflective, like the moon. Male/female is another pair of opposites which must be reconciled on this level. It is another polar paradox of the coincidence of opposites, like dark vs. light, deprivation vs. acquisition, emptiness vs. plenum, and transcendence vs. immanence.

The previous plate represented the ground of the Spirit; now we see the spiritual part of soul expressed through Immanence, which also transforms one's vision of the phenomenal world. The in-dwelling grace of God softens the old man's body. Immanence of the One in the creation permeates the world of nature so there is nothing in the world that is not God. This immanence is the soul in Nature, the *anima mundi*, the feminine Godhead.

The basic idea in God-mysticism is the return of the spirit to its immortal and infinite Ground, which is God. This is accomplished through rebirth in the spirit, the creation of an allegedly different creature. The highest state of mystic life is reached after the complete death of selfhood, past all images and intermediaries. Beyond nothingness, you lose, and simultaneously find yourself. The renunciate detaches and dies to egocentric life so the divine life may be born in the soul through union with the Godhead.

The Dark Night represents a way of negation, especially of any imagery. The *anima mundi* represents a way of affirmation and fullness. These two ways are not in opposition, rather they complement and supplement one another. Psychologically, the *anima* serves as a *mediatrix* for consciousness. She mediates between the personal and collective, balancing the actualities of daily life with the beyond.

Anima consciousness is a diffuse consciousness that is required for higher types of contemplation. The prayer spoken of in the text is mystical prayer, which is not verbal at all, but simply the most intense yearning of the soul to be united with God. This unification occurs without the intervention of reason or imagination, but by simple attention and humility, and self-forgetting. The Self is fully sunk in that which is One and All. St. Theresa of Avila created a metaphor between mystical prayer and ways of watering a garden: 1) using great effort to draw it up from a well; 2) using a windlass to get more water by less effort (stilling the senses); 3) using a river running through the garden (stilling the mind); and 4) God waters the garden with rain. Then the divine birth can take place in the human soul, as those like Meister Eckhart and Jacob Boehme testify.

This experience of *anima* is not a projection of a personal situation; nor is it a regressive clinging to the maternal. *Anima mundi* is the personification of the Soul. Ego-consciousness emerges as the result of her prior psychic life. The creative process emerges from the unconscious by way of the Mothers—rebirth. If your quest was initially for outward effectiveness, you have come to see your real need is for inner process work and process theology. You have found ways of using transformative symbols and images for your spiritual development.

Anima is archetype of the psyche. Since *Mercurius* is also archetype of the collective unconscious, there is an identity between *anima* and *Mercurius*. *Mercurius* contains a male and female aspect when representing the alchemical transformative agent. This *anima-Mercurius* is the factor through which all processes occur as "psychic."

The alchemist's conviction that psyche and its fantasies are as real as matter depends on how convincing *anima* has made herself to him. The turning inwards (digestion) from the object, in favor of internal images, is an experience of the *anima*—an internalization through sacrifice—quite necessary for psychic consciousness. Modern Jungians see consciousness itself as more appropriately based on *anima* than ego. The alchemist realizes that the ego and all its developmental fantasies and technologies never were the foundation for consciousness. Consciousness refers to a process that has more to do with images than will. It is reflection rather than control, with a reflective insight. Therefore, consciousness arising from soul derives from images and can be called imaginal. Its referent is myth as it manifests in life patterns, fantasies, and dreams.

At this state "becoming conscious" takes on new meaning. It means being aware of your fantasies and recognizing them everywhere including in your spiritual belief system. Your fantasies are not separate from your reality, but instrumental in forming your experience of it. The alchemist can suspend one state of consciousness for another. You can analyze by means of your fantasies and then translate reality back into fantasy images.

Personifying is a characteristic effect of the *anima* archetype. The embodiment of libido can only be apprehended in a definite form. Your rebirth is identical with your rebirth images, emotions, actions, feelings. This reborn or higher self is symbolized by the Holy Guardian Angel in the next plate. This Angel's individuation into a distinct personality is precisely what soul-making is about. This is the inner meaning of becoming conscious.

The entire choice between spirit and body, inner and outer, positive and negative has its source in identification with the ego. Ego maintains itself by creating conflict between the opposites within. It suppresses one and makes you believe you have chosen freely. Be sure your values and judgements are not based in the neurotic needs of an immature ego. *Anima* always presents striving consciousness with a moral dilemma, and at this phase the ego must stop its relentless climb to the spiritual summit and abide patiently. This dilemma is inherent in the nature of the ego, not the nature of *anima*.

We need to learn how to be in our souls, just like we had to reinhabit the body. Being-in-soul implies that you are being suffused with spirit. Their conjunction means spirit is reborn whenever you are in touch with soul. Just don't let your critical masculine voice undercut the experience by spiritualizing it into abstractions. Where the opposites dwell together there will be an interplay. Your inner male will try to extract meaning and carry it into action, invading your still beingness. *Anima* will intrude with images and distractions when you are working intellectually or focused in spiritual practice. Just watch the interplay without attachment. Let your imagination refresh your intellect with fantasy. Just preserve spirit and soul as distinct, but joined together. Let the spiritual energy direct your images toward the ultimate.

"The new Father brings forth a new Son"

PLATE 15

Here and now the sleeping Father,
Changes entirely into a clear water,
And through the power of the same water,
Now reaches a good property.

The new Father, strong and fine,
Also *brings forth a new Son*.
The Son remains fixed in the Father,
And the Father in the Son forever.

So different in all things,
They bring forth untold, precious fruit,
Which at no time may be corrupted,
And Death can destroy it no more.

They rest, through God's Grace,
Eternally in great triumph.

Father and Son sit on one throne;
The countenance of the Ancient Master
Is secured between them,
Hung with a crimson cloak.

The Father, Son and Guide now bound in Unity
Remain close together for eternity.

Only to God be the Praise and Glory

Amen

Chapter 15: Individuation and Rebirth

Rebirth

IN this final depiction of the alchemical Trinity, winged *Mercurius* is the spirit of the unconscious, the Holy Ghost. The last time all three figures appeared in the plates, the son was in the center. Now, the Divine takes its rightful place center-stage. The rebirth of the son marks the completion of the Great Work. This is an image of the Unitive life, the highest stage of mysticism. Another phase completes the second octave of transformation, but it is so ineffable it is not shown. Father, Son, and Guide now form a unity that is strongly reminiscent of Gnosticism.

Gnostics believe that the soul is a divine Spark which descends into physical manifestation for the sake of experience. There is initially an awareness of being a "stranger in a strange land" or life in an absurd universe filled with despair, anxiety, disgust, and fear. Salvation from this state comes through a revelation given by the grace of God, and it is an intuitive knowledge of the heart. The central religious experience of Gnosticism is inspiration and direction from one's guardian angel, which is considered identical with one's twin self or "divine self." There is a personal experience of encounter between the I, or ego, and divine self. They are distinct but share a fundamental unity. Feminine Wisdom is an inherent figure in Gnosticism embodied as Sophia. She is a companion of God and created the world. The Jews call her *Shekinah*.

These souls hasten back to their original spiritual home, aided by self-knowledge, which is a revelation of one's true self. Gnosis, as self-consciousness, shares much in common with the Jungian worldview, which is not a religion, but a sacred psychology. Both the path of Gnosis and individuation are processes of awakening the divine counterpart of the self and finally reintegrating in the bliss of the Pleroma or fullness of the spiritual world.

Gnostics believe in three aspects of humanity: 1) the body, as material or corporeal; 2) the soul, as an ethical awareness and power of reason; 3) and a spirit, which dreams unconsciously and is a divine spark of the same substance as Sophia and even God. In Christian Gnosticism, the final reunion is of each soul and its angel forming a Higher Self with Christ and Sophia in the Pleroma. This is considered a spiritual or sacred marriage, the complete union of the I and the Self.

The Unitive Life is the stabilization of the psychedelic and ecstatic revelations of the Illuminative phase. This is the final triumph of the spirit through attainment of a complete and permanent synthesis and reconciliation between the *within* and the *without*. Spiritual Marriage is the end result of following the Mystic Way. Death of selfhood leads to a complete and utter transformation of personality through a permanent change of consciousness.

The soul is fully united with That which is beyond all appearances, or is one with God. This is the final summit of the mystic mountain. The mystic realizes the Greater Self in its essentially eternal nature. It is the mystic's true nature, and he identifies with it, and so becomes Self. The mystic directly perceives that the basic stuff of the universe is Spirit; the Reality behind all phenomena is Spirit. There is nothing in the universe that is not God or everlasting Spirit. Everything lives in Spirit; it is the seed of all seeds; from it everything comes. This altered state of consciousness is permanent.

The stage where all aspects of self have been transcended is beyond words. Words are totally inadequate to express it. Paradoxical statements distort any descriptions of the ineffable experience. Still, all mystics describe the state in the same terms. The ideal of yoga is to live in the eternal present, free of the illusions of space, time, and the separate self. The liberated one no longer has a personal consciousness, but witnesses with spontaneity and lucidity as in "clear water." Taoist sages say that "Muddy water let stand becomes clear." Meditation stills the mind. The psyche dips down into space/time and the ego to experience cognitive consciousness, observe and experience nature, and co-create the world of experience. Every natural stage of human spiritual development leads it back to its celestial home.

Since the three illusions are properties of the normal state of consciousness, liberation is experienced only in altered states of consciousness. These higher altered states include several plateaus known in yoga as *jhana* states, meaning knowledge states. The psychedelic visions which accompany most of these *jhana* states are a psychological method of integration. *Jhanas 0–4* belong to the Illuminative phase.

> *Jhana 0* is a grace state initiating access beyond the bounds of time and space.
>
> *Jhana 1* occurs as an infusion of knowledge to the mind, and a moral illumination for the Self. The yogi commonly sees, as well as hears, God.
>
> In *Jhana 2* the yogi is touched by God, the Self is embodied spiritually. It is the first step in release from the prison of selfhood and a move

toward merging with ultimate reality. It is ecstatic and blissful. It is a Knowledge-Contact Ecstasy, a direct contact with the sacred. Rational thought and memory are suspended.

Jhana 3 is a Knowledge-Contact Ecstasy also, but one of direct knowing. Rapture and ecstasy cease. Hindus call it *Savicara Samadhi.*

Jhana 4 is the release of the Self through transcendence. It is the third degree of Knowledge-Contact and a process of absorption.

Jhana 5 belongs to the Unitive phase. It is characterized by ineffable contact, incommunicable knowledge, and consciousness of infinite space. Penetration of the psyche by the divine is changing into union.

Jhana 6 is transcendental contact or objectless infinite consciousness. Body, mind, and senses cease their restless motion, space melts away, the soul becomes lost in the Self beyond duality, beyond words, beyond thought.

Jhana 7 is an ineffable union; transmutation of the Self into Deity. Being and knowledge are undifferentiated. There is awareness of nothing-ness. This spiritual union is *Asampajnate Samadhi.*

The final Ineffable Union is *Jhana 8*, where there is neither perception nor nonperception. Words are useless here, but the triple prison of the three illusions of time, space, and ego is totally transcended. The Hindu yogi first concentrates on an object, grasps knowledge of its essence, then essentially becomes the object. The object is usually the Lord, devoid of association, grasped directly and leading to fusion. Human consciousness is eliminated by life in the eternal present. The soul is reabsorbed by the primordial substance and energy. These yogic states of escalation can be compared to the process of integration. The gist of the process is that when the individual comingles with the transpersonal field of Consciousness, duality is abolished, and through knowledge more and more complete, the one becomes the other.

All the great mystics speak of this omega point, when the All is in All without differentiation. This is the object of existence. Alchemically, it is steady-state liberation. Meister Eckhart expressed it as "I am become God" in the closest semantic translation. In Lambsprinck, the guide is revealed as the ancient Master, and the disciple and Master have become one forever. This integration is the final realization of the regenerative process. It is the end of human becoming and the start of *being* a whole human being.

This state of integration is the psychological equivalent of salvation, the heavenly estate. Development has taken place on seven levels: physical, emotional, mental, relational, creative, intuitive, and spiritual. It is the goal of the human evolutionary, developmental process. Paradoxically, the Unitive state is also a naturally occurring, spontaneous, transitory state that can manifest in any moment of ego-loss. This consciousness is the more rare complement of dualism. It is the foundation of contemplative spirituality. It is intuition, mystery, pure being. Symbolically, it is experienced as a childlike realization that your consciousness is single and immortal. You experience yourself as a divine, transcendent soul, which remains untouched by time. Thus, the rebirth is accomplished, through God's grace, and time seems to stand still. It is a gift of God, not the result of effort.

Abraham Maslow evoked memories of spontaneous peak experiences by asking about a person's most ecstatic moment in life. What was yours? You may recall some unitive states by recalling an experience in which time seemed suspended, you were caught up in forgetfulness of self, but you felt wide-awake, open, and lucid. When you cease self-defining activities during sex, intimacy, spiritual discipline, or appreciation of nature or the arts, you have changed "into a clear water."

In his comments on the Unitive experience in *Will and Spirit*, Gerald May echoed the Lambsprinck metaphor several times:

> The ideal meditative state according to many spiritual traditions is one in which awareness is both very wide-awake and open, where the water is calm, clear, and still. . . . Using the water analogy again, meditation masters often say that any effort to still the waves only creates more waves. Therefore, meditation must ideally be a situation in which trying stops and things are allowed to settle into their natural state. . . All the senses are acute, but there is no mental labeling or reaction concerning sensory stimuli. The water is very clear and calm. . . . They [Unitive experiences] are the simplicity that remains after all self-defining activities are temporarily suspended. What is then perceived is raw and unadulterated, a reflection of things-just-as-they-are in an utterly natural state: clear water.

When experiencing spontaneous unity, there is no self-reflection, no awe or wonder. The feeling reaction comes when you begin to lose the experience. It is a feeling of truth, rightness, freedom, warmth, expansiveness, pure love. These transient experiences can go unnoticed if they are subtle. Many times their memory is repressed because the characteristic feeling of self-loss is too scary or overwhelming to the ego. But even these brief moments of "at-one-ment" feed the longing for reunion.

It may manifest as an emotional nostalgia, or a committed spiritual search. Many times a fleeting unitive experience is what sparks a seeker's spiritual awakening. However, some seekers become confused and think they are in unity when they are enmeshed in dualism, frequently oriented around the issue of good/bad. Others try to goad themselves into unitive experiences, which simply cannot be done.

Gerald May characterizes the Unitive state of mind as one which usually goes unnoticed since most of recognized time is spent in a dualistic state:

> The unitive state occurs less frequently and lasts less long. At least that is the way it is in most people's experience. The validity of this observation is open to some question, because unitive experiences can essentially be noticed only after the fact. And they must be remembered to be acknowledged. If during a unitive experience one begins to identify what is happening, the experience must stop. Any comment or observation about what is occurring is a self-defining act that by its nature must disrupt the unitive state of mind. In contrast, duality can be observed readily and immediately, in the moment while it is happening.

The final Lambsprinck plate depicts a final process of distillation in which the Stone of the Philosophers is fixed. At last, after a long period of transformation, equilibrium is established with the Soul acting as channel between Spirit and Matter. This culminating illustration has harmonizing meanings on the four levels:

Spiritual Level: The Unitive life. The achievement of the purpose of evolution; the incorruptible Body governed by Spiritual principle. This marks the successful end of the individuation process at a cosmic level. A saint or Master-soul embodies the Spirit united and fixed in the material body through the medium of the soul. The two poles of divergently manifesting power, Spirit as energy and Matter as form, are in balance.

Mental Level: Illumination of the mind rid of mental blockages that act as resistances against perfection. Consequently, the mind can call on infinite resources. Intuition and Knowledge are in correct functional balance. Cognitive/creative balance. Absorptive states of increasing power and clarity. Integration.

Emotional Level: Conscience is the result of a thought/feeling integration. The elemental forces behind emotions are correctly and appropriately channeled, and the emotional structure is purified of emotional blockages. Head and heart unite. Blessedness. Empathy, rapport.

Physical Level: The "ethereal body" is realized through the mind/body integration. The dynamic, circulative energy of the spiritual body is experienced. The physical body is now perfected and in harmony; disease caused by wrong attitudes no longer manifests the effects of unbalance in the "Temple of the Spirit."

In alchemy, the number four represents wholeness, five represents essence (quintessence). The fourfold process of distillation is completed through the production of the quintessence. Thus man's nature is purified and refined through successive stages. Spirit has sought consciousness of itself through material manifestation—the cycle of devolution and evolution is complete. A review of the alchemical distillations shows how the fifth state is also the One:

First Stage: The gross matter (Man) is placed in the vessel and heat is applied. Although they are not visible, the gross Matter also contains Soul and Spirit. Correspondences include the element earth, winter, life on earth, the process of maturing, and night. Identification of the problem.

Second Stage: In time the Spirit and Soul leave the gross Matter due to the action of heat. The natural process of heat terminates the life of the gross matter. Correspondences include the element air, the process of meditation, "letting go," death, the threshold, the process of withdrawal into new conditions, and dawn.

Third Stage: The Spirit arrives at the top of the Vessel having left behind the coarser material of the Soul. It has arrived at its natural home. Correspondences include the element of fire, awareness of the unity of heaven embracing the Spirit, the process of rest and latency, and resurrection. New vision. Daytime.

Fourth Stage: The Spirit condenses and begins to fall back to the gross Matter. In pursuit of its task of obtaining a correct attitude in material conditions, the Spirit returns through the mental and emotional worlds and creates a body and environment suitable to its stage of evolution and karma. Correspondences include the element water, birth, incarnation, and evening. Actualization.

The fifth stage is also the first. The unitive experience, which originally led to spiritual awakening and seeking, is that same state of mind which is stabilized into steady-state enlightenment. It corresponds with the ether, rebirth, suspension of time, immortality, reincarnation, pure Being. The alchemist Gerhard Dorn speaks of the spirit/body union and healing water in *Theatrum Chemicum* (1602):

> Learn therefore, O Mind, to practice sympathetic love in regard to thine own body, by restraining its vain appetites, that it may be apt with thee in all things. To this end I shall labour, that it may drink with thee from the fountain of strength, and, when the two are made one, that ye find peace in their union. Draw nigh, O Body, to this fountain, that with thy Mind thou mayest drink to satiety and thirst no more after vanities. O wondrous efficacy of this fount, which maketh one of two, and peace between enemies! The fount of love can make *mind* out of spirit and soul, but this maketh *one man* of mind and body.

In the final Lambsprinck plate, the father (body) and son (spirit) are joined in unity, and will remain so for ever more. The winged old man is *Mercurius* in the form of the God of Revelation. He is identical with Hermes Trimegistus, patron of the Great Work. With the king and the king's son, he completes the alchemical Trinity, equivalent to Father, Son, and Holy Spirit.

Individuation is Jung's term for a system of personal psychic transformation. The process culminates in a grand reunion of archetypal opposites, producing the state of wholeness. It is the apex of the process of becoming or spiritual development and the beginning of being. The dynamics of individuation involve a dialogue between consciousness and the unconscious Self. It proceeds through a thesis being attacked by antithesis. This is the basis of the I-Self relationship. It yields a synthesis on a higher level of consciousness.

In alchemy the process is symbolized by warring opposites, which in the end come to peaceful reconciliation. The dualities of existence are harmonized as complementary, not antagonistic, opposites. During the process they consume each other, eventually yielding the perfect product: the regenerative union of the Body, Soul, and Spirit. There are two distinct phases of individuation as represented in Lambsprinck's work:

1) The first stage is the work of the *soul*. Its modality is *metamorphosis*, qualitative change. It involves progressive differentiation of the ego from its original unity with the Self. This process is facilitated by

therapy. Its goal is empowerment and self-actualization. It is a "tuning-up" of personality.

2) The second stage relates to the *spirit*. Its modality is *transformation* and *personification*, or embodiment of spirit. The ego seeks to abandon personal power for the deeper reward of gaining knowledge, contact, and identification with the Self, in a conscious way. This process is facilitated by spiritual practice such as *meditation*. Its goal is Self-realization and God-realization. It is the purification and absorption of the whole individual in the Divine.

Individuation is a spontaneous process within the psyche. It is a natural part of the human growth process that continues throughout life. It seems to have an evolutionary element. It is possible to become consciously aware of this process through the observation of dreams, behavior, belief systems, and imagery. Working with the process seems to facilitate its unfolding. This is not without peril, so it is not an advisable spiritual path for all. Individuation is the psychological equivalent of initiation. Individuation is one path for those who choose to realize their essence through direct personal experience of the Divine Source.

Individuation is the goal of spiritual psychology. It leads to a form of rebirth within an individual lifespan. It is a renewal brought about through an essentially alchemical procedure. The refining of the personality leads to changes in its function, but not in its essential nature. This final stage represents a spontaneous, metaphysical experiential state where the alchemist unites with the Guardian Angel as Master. This produces an enlargement of personality through enhanced consciousness of resources which flow from within oneself.

Consciousness can experience transformation by submitting itself to this alchemical technique. This technical process is a "speeding up" or elaboration of the natural process available through contemplation, introspection, concentration, and meditation. Meditation is done for the sake of entering a state of being, stillness, sacred emptiness. But it is not performed compulsively by seeking more and more unitive absorptions. It is a time each day to surrender self-defining beliefs and activities, break free of limitations, and experience expansion in the greater whole.

The larger and greater personality that matures within you is the inner friend of the soul. You somehow perceive this inner directing voice guiding you through many changes. It is quite natural and is recounted in the lives of saints and prophets throughout history. This internal dialogue with the inner Master is the alchemical form of meditation. The ego and the body grant proper valuation to the guidance of the Self. In the final plate, the Self is "hung with a crimson cloak." This crimson-colored cloak alludes to the mystery nature of blood. To medieval Lambsprinck, it must have related to the transubstantiation in the Mass. As one consumes the Divine substance, one identifies with and becomes That. Uniting with this Angel, the Self, is the key to immortality.

The Angel may manifest in many ways other than inner dialogue. Frequently the response appears synchronistically as the action of an outward agent. The alchemists saw this in the transformation of the chemical substance. As they sought transformation, they discovered it outside themselves in matter. These transformations also affected them personally, but had an impersonal, transpersonal aspect, as well. The transformation was not a personal achievement. Alchemists performed incomprehensible experiments, but somehow they were able to demonstrate how ego-consciousness reacts to the superior guidance of the Self using metaphor, symbol, and image. In the spiritual sense, the alchemists learned what was mortal and immortal. Then they sought to identify with the immortal by seeking the Source.

The intuition of immortality is connected with the peculiar nature of the unconscious. It is a realm of experience that is nonlinear, nonspatial, and nontemporal. At very advanced levels of spiritual perception, it appears alternately as an absolute Void and as a Plenum, full of the richness of the heights and the depths. The Angel is the embodiment of the Self, a messenger from the Divine Source. As friend, advisor, comforter, and teacher of revealed wisdom, the Angel as Master of the individual rules benevolently. The fruits of the state of blessedness are abundant.

Chapter 16: Master or God-Man

Ultima Materia

THE Great Work culminates in that paragon of evolution—the fully developed and mature Man or Woman. Both masculine and feminine qualities are balanced and harmonized. This God-Man represents the fully ripened fruit of the Tree of Life. A master soul has attained spiritual perfection by immersing himself in the divine stream to find union with God. He is one with the Limitless Light. Therefore, no symbolic picture or image of this phase is possible. It is the Clear Light.

What kind of individual exemplifies this stage of attainment? This is the level of the God-realized individual, or one who has unsealed the soul and untied the knots that bind it. The living saint is a son or daughter of God. In the Jewish faith, they are known as *zaddik* or *sadek*. Each "saint-in-training" had a spiritual teacher, known as *maggid*, who had passed through the same path. These saints were not born but made, partly by the assistance of God and partly by their own efforts. But no matter how brave they were, they always needed a guide. However, they did not model their behavior after one another; rather, they expressed their individuality most authentically.

Lambsprinck was a Christian kabbalist. Kabbalah is an ancient Jewish mystical search for union with the Divine. Masters of the Kabbalah taught the techniques of meditation and preparation for ecstasy that could lead to union with God. They taught concentration and contemplation on the Hebrew names of God, which could free the individual to move toward true mystical ecstasy.

In India, such a saint who is also a teacher is called a Satguru, or true Guru, to distinguish him from the many lower levels of false prophets, teachers, and yogis. The Master has a perfect understanding of his relationship to the universe. Like the kabbalists, he teaches repetition of the names of God, contemplation, meditation, and soul travel. He teaches the path of the Masters. He is a living embodiment of his teaching. His teachings integrate ancient meditation techniques into modern life. He is an instrument of the divine, who immerses himself in the divine Stream ("clear water"), finds union, and teaches his followers to do the same. Helping others free themselves before proceeding to the ultimate unification is the mission of the Buddhist *Bodhisattvas* or World Saviors.

The real savior during this whole process is the Self, as an individualized representative of divinity. It is this conscious awareness of Self which is born out of the process of integration. Paradoxically, it initiated the process in the beginning, serving as the driving impulse behind it. So, the Self gives birth to the Self. It refines the personality until it is a fit vehicle for a higher order of consciousness. No one has an individual Self. The Self is the same Self in all individuals. The Hindus call it *Atman*.

However, the Self always regenerates itself in an individualized form. The transpersonal energy uses human individuality as its channel and tool. Not all integrated persons are prophets or saints, only the most gifted. But all possess sagely wisdom, compassion, and engagement in life. This phase is beyond all dialogical dualism (I-Thou). The richness of inner life is experienced as celestial exaltation and effulgence like Clear Light.

Appendix

A Note on
The Book of Lambsprinck

THE origins of the *The Book of Lambsprinck* are veiled in mystery. It arose from the school of Hermetic alchemy which climaxed as a formal art tradition in the sixteenth and seventeenth centuries. The manuscript itself dates from 1599 when a Latin translation of the German version appeared, without the engravings, in the *Triga chemica* published by Nicholas Barnaud in Leiden, Germany.

Lambsprinck's *De lapide philosophico* was first published with the seventeen copperplate engravings in 1625 and later reprinted in the *Museum Hermeticum* (1678). The illustrations were created and first published by the famous Belgian family of engravers, the de Brys.

Of Protestant derivation, the de Bry family was forced to relocate in Frankfurt because of the political climate of the day. Their talent was channeled into a successful engraving business by Theodor de Bry, who died in 1610. Of his two sons, Johann Theodor de Bry rose to position and entertained such personages as Robert Fludd and Michael Maier (*Atalanta Fugiens*). It is now believed that Johann Theodor de Bry embellished the words of Lambsprinck. The 1625 edition was published by Lucas Jennis, the stepson of Johann Israel de Bry, Johann Theodor de Bry's younger brother.

Aside from the tradition that the philosopher Lambsprinck was German, little is known of him. Such was often the case with many great writers during this period. The alchemists set out to reveal while simultaneously obscuring their truth, actual techniques, and methodologies. To escape charges of heresy, they often concealed their true identities. Lambsprinck may be a figure of fiction, used to cloak the teachings, an archetypal example of the alchemist. Indeed, according to Stanislas Klossowski de Rola in his book *The Golden Game: Alchemical Engravings of the Seventeenth Century*, "the name of the author is an obvious pseudonym, underlined by the coat-of-arms designed to attract attention to Aries and to the spring."

Many references have been made to Lambsprinck's work *On the Stone of the Philosophers*. Carl Jung, for example, refers to Lambsprinck in many of his *Collected Works*, including *Psychology and Alchemy* and *Alchemical*

Studies. Other works include C. A. Burland's *The Arts of the Alchemists* (1967), Hans Biedermann's *Handlexicon der Magischen Kunste* (1973), and David William's *The Book of Lambspring* (1972). Today, an English translation of the *Hermetic Museum* by A. E. Waite is still in print and available from Samuel Weiser. Other forms of this work also exist. For example, R.A.M.S. Press published *Lambspring's Process,* based on a translation from the German by Sigismund Bacstrom (1804). This differs radically from the original text and focuses primarily on the laboratory aspects and processes.

Bibliography

Frater Albertus. *The Alchemist's Handbook*. York Beach: Samuel Weiser, 1987.

Boehme, Jacob. *The Way to Christ*. Translated by Peter Erb. New York: Paulist Press, 1978.

Brown, Molly Young. *The Unfolding Self*. Los Angeles: Psychosynthesis Press, 1983.

Buber, Martin. *I and Thou*. Translated by Walter Kaufmann. New York: Paulist Press, 1978.

Burland, C. A. *The Arts of the Alchemists*. New York: Macmillan, 1968.

Cockren, A. *Alchemy Rediscovered and Restored*. London: Rider, 1940.

Corbin, Henry. *Spiritual Body and Celestial Earth*. Princeton: Princeton University Press, 1977.

Dychtwald, Ken. *Bodymind*. Los Angeles: J. P. Tarcher, 1977.

Edinger, Edward F. *Anatomy of the Psyche*. La Salle: Open Court, 1985.

Eliade, Mircea. *The Forge and The Crucible: The Origins and Structure of Alchemy*. Chicago: University of Chicago Press, 1979.

Ferruci, Piero. *What We May Be*. Los Angeles: J. P. Tarcher, 1982.

Gowan, John Curtis. *Trance, Art, and Creativity*. Northridge: Creative Education Foundation, 1975.

Grinnell, Robert. *Alchemy in a Modern Woman*. Dallas: Spring Publications, 1973.

Grof, Stanislov. *The Adventure of Self-Discovery*. New York: State University of New York Press, 1988.

Grosinger, Richard. *The Alchemical Tradition in the Late Twentieth Century*. Berkeley: North Atlantic Books, 1979.

Happold, F. C. *Mysticism: A Study and an Anthology*. Hamondsworth: Penguin, 1971.

Harding, M. Esther. *Psychic Energy: Its Source and its Transformation*. Princeton: Princeton University Press, 1973.

Hillman, James. *Re-Visioning Psychology*. New York: Harper and Row, 1975.

Holmyard, E. J. *Alchemy*. New York: Penguin, 1968.

Jung, C. G. *Alchemical Studies*. Princeton: Princeton University Press, 1967.

————. *Psychology and Alchemy*. Princeton: Princeton University Press, 1968.

————. *Mysterium Coniunctionis*. Princeton: Princeton University Press, 1970.

Klossowski de Rola, Stanislas. *Alchemy: The Secret Art*. London: Thames and Hudson, 1973.

————. *The Golden Game: Alchemical Engravings of the Seventeenth Century*. London: Thames and Hudson, 1988.

May, Gerald G. *Will And Spirit: A Contemplative Psychology*. San Francisco: Harper and Row, 1987.

Neumann, Erich. *The Origins and History of Consciousness*. Princeton: Princeton University Press, 1954.

Paracelsus. *The Hermetic and Alchemical Writings of Paracelsus*. Translated by A. E. Waite. Edmonds: Alchemical Press, 1991.

Progoff, Ira. *The Symbolic and the Real*. New York: McGraw-Hill, 1963.

Rulandus, Martinus. *A Lexicon of Alchemy or Alchemical Dictionary*. London: James Elliott, 1893. Reprint. York Beach: Samuel Weiser, 1984.

Sanford, John. *Healing and Wholeness*. New York, Paulist Press, 1977

————. *Dreams and Healing*. New York: Paulist Press, 1978.

————. *The Invisible Partners*. New York: Paulist Press, 1980.

Singer, June. *Boundaries of the Soul*. Garden City: Doubleday, 1973.

von Franz, Marie-Louise. *Alchemical Active Imagination*. Dallas: Spring Publications, 1979.

————. *Alchemy: An Introduction to the Symbolism and the Psychology*. Toronto: Inner City Books, 1980.

Waite, Arthur Edward, translator. *The Hermetic Museum*. York Beach: Samuel Weiser, 1991.

————. *The Turba Philosophorum, or Assembly of the Sages*. London: George Redway, 1896. Reprint. New York: Samuel Weiser, 1970.

Walsh and Shapiro, editors. *Beyond Health and Normality*. New York: Van Nostrand Reinhold, 1983.

Washburn, Michael. *Ego and the Dynamic Ground*. Albany: State University of New York Press, 1988.

Wilber, Ken. *The Atman Project*. Wheaton: Quest Books, 1980.

————. *No Boundary*. Boulder: Shambhalla, 1981.

Woodman, Marion. *The Ravaged Bridegroom*. Toronto: Inner City Books, 1990.

Index

Abandonment, 30, 100, 121, 137, 187, 188
Abyss, 77, 78, 97, 190
Addiction, 98, 99, 153
Adversary, 63, 69, 70
Air, 87, 90, 95, 133, 140
Albedo, 97, 98, 101,103
Alchemy, 9, 10, 13, 24, 55, 87, 104–106, 134–135, 165, 175, 178, 207, 213
Alexander, 61
Alpha and Omega, 151, 203
Ambivalence, 47, 67
American Dream, the, 30
Amrita, 192
Androgyny, 56, 122, 152, 164, 179
Angel, 11, 147, 154, 161, 166, 168–169, 176, 195, 201, 209. *See also* Holy Guardian Angel
Anima, 13, 27, 45–51, 55, 63, 69, 81, 102, 104, 166, 170, 193, 195, 196; anima consciousness 185, 195
Anima Mundi, 77, 78, 117, 193, 194
Animus, 13, 27, 49, 50, 55–57, 59, 63, 69, 120, 151
Apocalypse, 65
Archetype(s), 14, 15, 26–27, 45, 55, 58, 68, 79–80, 91, 103, 121–122, 129, 138, 151, 169, 179
Aristotle, 129
Armor, 29
Art, 18, 43, 46, 53, 55, 101, 115, 121, 129, 136, 154–155
Artemis, 103
Atman, 212
Augmentation, 131
Augustus, 43
Awakening, 35, 39–40, 111

Bacchus, 152
Balm, 73, 80, 141, 186, 192
Baphomet, 69
Base matter, 23
Basilisk, 73
Bisexuality, 153

Bird(s), 84–85, 87, 94–95, 97–98, 104
Birth, 89, 90, 121
Black, blackness, 32–35, 38, 95, 98, 103
Black hole, 66
Blood, 131, 209
Bly, Robert, 99
Bodhisattva, 211
Body, 50, 56–57, 61, 63–64, 66, 75–78, 81, 88, 97, 99, 100–101, 103–104, 111, 118, 133, 136, 139, 145, 147, 151, 155, 161–163, 166, 169, 175, 177, 183, 191, 203, 206–208
Body of Light, 111
Boehme, Jacob, 194
Broch, Hermann, 129
Butterfly, 164

Caduceus, 104
Calcinatio, 14, 133
Campbell, Joseph, 31, 112, 121
Chakra(s), 90, 101, 118, 166
Chaos, 78, 106, 121, 122, 154
Charisma, 141, 142
Chi, 141
Child, divine. *See* Divine child
Circle, 164
Circulatio, 14, 165
Circulation, 90, 165, 166
Clairvoyance, 40
Clear Light, 211, 212
Clear water, 199, 202, 211
Clouds, 191
Coagulatio, 14, 75–82, 87, 98, 101, 133, 165
Codependence, 29, 133, 135
Collective unconscious, 24, 29, 77, 89
Compensation, 105
Complex(es), 13, 14, 29, 48, 49, 69, 81, 126, 136, 137, 140
Conception, 82, 175–180
Conflict, 24, 28, 36, 45–48, 64, 69, 81, 97, 98, 105–106, 118, 122, 150, 179, 195
Coniunctio, 14, 50, 97, 106, 107, 117,

120, 136
Consciousness, 76, 81, 88, 97, 98,
    101, 103, 105, 111–112, 117–118,
    120–121, 125, 133, 135, 139, 148,
    150, 161, 167, 176, 193, 195, 204,
    206
Consciousness, cosmic, 27, 112, 118,
    133, 156, 164
Contemplation, 101
Covalent bonding, 45
Creativity, 51, 57, 70, 106, 111, 118,
    123, 126, 128, 135, 152
Critic, inner, 40
Crone, 82
Crown, 53
Crucifixion, 123

Darkness, 38, 47, 52, 53, 55, 65–66,
    77, 99, 120, 127, 187–188, 190,
    193
Dark night of the soul, 185–6, 191,
    194
Death, 45, 65, 73, 75, 81, 90, 95, 131,
    133, 135, 139–140, 143, 177, 189,
    194, 199
Death/rebirth, 75, 81, 89, 98, 125,
    177, 186, 206
Denial, 47, 126
Depression, 28, 35, 37–38, 39, 40, 47,
    133, 149, 153
Dialogue, 12, 24, 31, 38, 46, 80, 139,
    140, 154, 159, 163, 166, 207–209
Diamond, 103, 138
Diamond body, 139, 154
"Die daily," 75, 191
Dismemberment, 69, 90
Dissociation, 89
Dissolution, 69
Distillation, 88, 99, 161, 175, 206
Divination, 141
Divine child, 119, 149, 151–152
Divorce, 35
Dog, 60–61, 63–64, 66, 68, 103
Dolphin, 117
Doors of perception, 161
Dove, 95, 97–98, 101–103
Dragon, 32, 33, 35–37, 55, 72 –73, 75,
    77, 79, 114, 117, 122
Dream(s), 10–12, 14, 23–24, 37, 48–
    49, 51, 65, 67, 70, 81–82, 103, 117,
    134–135, 137–142, 148–149, 151–

52, 154, 195–196
Dreamwork, 134

Earth, 81, 122, 133, 140, 147, 164,
    166, 192
Earthquake, 65
Ecstasy, 27, 124, 156, 164, 177, 211
Ego, 12, 24–29, 36, 37, 39, 45, 48–49,
    55, 63, 66–69, 75–78, 80–81, 88,
    97, 100–102, 105, 119–120, 122–
    123, 125, 133, 138–139, 147, 153,
    161, 171, 195, 202
Ego consciousness, 99, 194–209
Ego death, 25, 75, 90, 11, 120, 135
Egypt, 87, 180
Einstein, Albert, 111
Eleusinian mysteries, 152
Elixer, 139
Elixer vitae, 185
Emptiness, 189–190, 192, 194
Enantiodromia, 47
Enlightenment, 88, 118, 120, 143,
    148, 176, 207
Eros, 106
ESP, 40
"Ethereal body," 206
Evil, 37, 45, 65–66, 69, 99, 106, 120,
    127, 192

Falling, 81
False prophet, 91
Father, 85, 118, 144–145, 147, 149,
    159, 165, 172–173, 175, 182, 183,
    185, 198–199, 201, 207
Fear, 111, 132, 151, 187
Fertility, 81
Fire, 73, 77, 82, 85, 98, 104–105, 130–
    131, 133, 135–137, 140, 179, 185–
    186, 206
Fire-bath, 136
Fish, 20–21, 25–26
Flood, flooding, 65–66, 68
Folie à deux, 58
Forest, 42–43, 45, 72–73, 75, 85, 95,
    104, 114–115, 117
Fragmentation, 106, 152
Freud, Sigmund, 66

Genius, 99, 101, 128–129

Gnosticism, 201
Gnostics, 201
God, 12, 17–18, 23, 33, 61, 85, 95, 112, 115, 120, 125, 127, 131, 136, 141, 143, 147, 151, 154, 157, 163, 171, 175–176, 178, 180, 183, 185–190, 194, 202, 211
Goddess, 77, 81, 82, 99
God-image, 161–171
God-man, 211–212
God-realization, 167, 208, 211
Gold, 23, 103, 115, 139
Golden Fleece, 43
Golden Mean, 46
Good, 37, 45, 65–66, 69, 78, 82, 106, 117, 119, 120, 124, 127, 192
Grace, 13, 16, 40, 124, 126, 143, 156, 166, 176–177, 183, 185, 188, 190–191, 199, 201, 204
Grail, 121
Grail King, 185
Great Goddess, 63
Great Mother, 27, 63, 75, 77–78, 81–82, 119, 122, 141
Great Work, 14, 26, 67, 80, 101, 139, 151, 167, 171, 178, 191, 201, 207, 211
Grof, Stanislav, 90
Guardian angel. See Holy Guardian Angel
Guide, 11, 13, 118, 144–145, 147–149, 154, 158–159, 161, 165, 168, 170–171, 179, 201
Guru, 11, 91, 125, 167, 170

Hallaj, 119
Hallucinations, 66
Healer, 27, 140–141, 148, 179
Healing, 10, 23, 25, 69, 80, 97–99, 101–102, 104, 118, 127, 135, 137, 138, 140–142, 150, 192, 207
Heart, 145
Hegel, 46
Hermes, Hermes Trimegistus, 87, 115, 179, 207
Hermetic philosophy, 11
Hermetic vessel, 49, 166
Hero, 117, 119, 121–122, 124
Higher Power, 100–112, 124, 156, 162
Higher Self, 23, 126, 135, 141, 163–

164, 167, 170, 176, 201
High priestess, 63
Hillman, James, 129, 193
Hologram, 138
Holy Ghost, 177–178, 180, 201
Holy Guardian Angel, 49, 104, 125, 140, 154, 195, 208
Holy Spirit, 135, 185, 189, 191

Iacchus, 153
Icarus, 152
I Ching, 117, 141
Identity, 31, 57, 118, 128, 134, 140, 179
Illumination, 27, 40, 118, 126, 133, 202
Illuminative way, 187, 202
Imagery, 13, 24, 57, 66, 82, 112, 123, 134, 139, 151, 157, 194, 208
Imagination, 11, 13, 14, 26, 39, 48, 55, 57, 67, 77, 81–82, 102, 104, 136, 141, 162, 167, 169, 190, 196
Immortality, 82, 119, 135, 136, 139, 154, 175, 192–193
Incubation, 185–196
India, 95, 104, 159, 166, 170, 192, 211
Individuation, 9, 11, 26, 28, 35, 38, 63, 80–81, 123, 139, 207–208
Inflation, 141, 153
Initiation, 82, 123, 133–135, 137, 143
Inner child, 27, 137, 152
Inner dialogue, 24, 38
Inner guide, 49, 55, 165, 168
Inner mate, 49, 50, 63
Integrity, 26
Intellect, 24, 28, 37, 39, 121, 188, 190, 196
Intoxication, 152
Intuition, 107, 136, 140, 151, 161, 204, 205, 209
Invocation, 138
Isis, 63, 81

Jacob's ladder, 148
Jesus Christ, 17, 151, 177
Jhana(s), 202–203
John of the Cross, 185, 187–190, 192
Jonah, 121, 189
Judge, 24, 40, 47, 48
Judgement, 39, 45, 135
Jung, Carl, 9–11, 24, 27, 35, 47, 48,

51, 119–120, 141, 150, 154–155,
  166, 207, 213
Jungian psychology, 24, 50, 91, 102,
  129

Kabbalah, 11, 211
Kali, 77
Karma, 121, 191, 206
King, 114, 115, 117, 119, 122, 124–
  125, 147–148
King Arthur, 120
King Sol, 117, 118, 121, 136
Kundalini, 90, 104, 166

Ladder, 148, 164
Lambsprinck, 11, 16, 45, 49, 105–
  107, 111, 118, 128, 148, 150–
  151,162, 166–167, 177, 180, 187,
  191, 203–204, 207, 209, 211–214
Lead, 21, 23
Leo, 138
Levi, Eliphas, 69, 78
Libido, 69, 106, 133, 136–137
Lifestyle, 30, 89, 97, 121, 133
Light, 39, 47, 65, 78, 79, 81, 90, 99,
  117, 119, 121, 127, 139, 147, 162,
  165–166, 175, 180, 186. See also
  Clear Light
Lioness, 55
Lions, 52 –53, 55, 63, 103, 120, 138
Logos, 106, 175, 193
Loyola, Ignatius, 193
Lucid dream, 135
Luna, 102

Magic, 9, 87, 142, 143
Magical Child, 147, 150–151
Magician, 63, 92, 100, 121, 142
Mana personality, 91, 121, 126, 131–
  143, 151
Maslow, Abraham, 12, 161, 204
Master, 43, 92, 167, 170, 178, 199,
  203, 205, 208–209, 211
Matter, 10, 13–15, 21, 25, 43, 53, 64,
  88, 95, 97–99, 101–102, 104–105,
  123, 136, 141, 147, 165, 173, 175,
  177, 206
May, Gerald, 204, 205
Maya, 56

Medicine, 61, 80–81, 115, 131, 133,
  136
Meditatio, 166
Meditation, 13, 51, 67, 82, 88, 90,
  111–112, 120, 124–128, 136–137,
  139, 143, 148, 155, 156, 162, 164–
  165, 170, 175–176, 178, 186, 191,
  193, 208
Megalomania (gradiosity), 39, 141,
  153
Meister Eckhart, 194, 203
Melancholy, 149
Mephistopheles, 13
Mercurius, 179–180, 195, 201, 207
Mercury, 73, 85, 88
Meru, Mount, 170
Metaphor, 209
Middle Pillar, 46
Middle Way, 46, 48
Midlife, 56, 127, 153
Mind/body split, 29, 77
Mood swings, 46, 48, 56
Moon, 81–82, 102–103, 136, 161, 193
Morality, 66, 77, 89
Mortificatio (mortification), 64, 187,
  190
Mysticism, 106, 124, 201
Mystics, 75, 78, 87, 92, 112, 119, 125,
  128, 180, 202
Myth, 24, 78, 112, 121, 129, 140, 185,
  195

Nature, 115, 128, 147, 156–157, 162,
  194
Nest, 84–85, 87
Neurosis, 136, 142
Nightmares, 37
Nigredo, 35–38, 40, 46, 101–102

Observer Self, 56
Oedipus, 121
Oil, 183
Opposites (pairs of, union of), 12, 26,
  45, 47–48, 55–56, 59, 63, 67, 97,
  104–106, 122, 127, 136, 171, 192–
  194, 207
Original sin, 25
Orr, Leonard, 90
Oscillations, 47, 56, 66, 105, 107

Pain, 75, 88, 125, 135, 137, 189
Panacea, 67, 134
Paranoia, 65, 89, 111
Participation mystique, 55–59, 64, 92, 102
Paul, Saint, 9
Peak (mountain), 145, 147
Peak experience, 12, 133, 148, 156, 161–162, 165
Pearls, 103, 115
Persia, 61
Persona, 23, 27, 29, 30, 31
Personality, 23, 48, 58, 65, 67, 79, 81, 97–98, 101, 105, 111, 117, 119, 121, 134–135, 140, 148, 154, 165
Personification, 82, 195, 208
Philosopher king, 118–119
Philosopher's Stone, 14, 80, 95, 97, 106, 131, 135–136, 139, 151, 154, 185, 205
Phobias, 65
Phoenix, 87, 95, 97–98, 104
Pineal, 192
Plenum, 192, 194, 209
Pleroma, 201
Pneuma, 90
Poison, 61, 67, 72–73, 75, 79
Prana, 90, 141
Prayer, 127
Pregnancy, 82
Presence, 126, 139, 156–157, 164
Pride, 127–128
Prima materia, 14, 23, 25–28, 64, 133, 151, 165
Prince, 147
Priest, 63
Process theology, 124, 143, 194–195
Projection, 39, 50–51, 57–59, 63, 67, 70, 133, 136, 139–141, 178, 194
Prophecy, 101
Psyche, 50, 97, 101, 105, 117, 120–121, 127, 135, 139, 166, 195, 208
Psyche (mythological figure), 147
Psychosynthesis, 107, 133, 139
Puella aeterna, 153
Puer aeternus, 120, 128
Puer/senex complex, 14, 120, 147–157
Purgation, 126, 135, 180, 185–190
Purification, 69, 87, 90, 98, 101, 190, 193, 206, 208
Putrefaction, 33

Rain, 183, 191–193
Raven, 33, 36
Rebel, 48, 154
Rebirth, 11, 29, 48, 64, 78, 82, 89, 98, 156, 175, 180, 183, 193–194, 201–209
Red, 94, 95, 97, 101, 104
Refinement, 133
Regeneration, 47, 51, 64, 75, 87, 97, 100, 104, 131, 134, 212
Resurrection, 64, 66, 165, 193
Rhythmic breathing, 90
Right livelihood, 179
Rubedo, 97–98, 101, 104

Sacred marriage, 50, 63, 97, 201
Sacrifice, 65, 135–136, 191
Salamander, 130–131, 133–134, 136–137, 140
Samadhi, 143, 156, 203
Sat Guru, 170, 211
Saturation, 61
Saturn, 78, 177
Saturn return, 35
Sea, 20–21
Seed of the metals, 17
Seeker, 9, 28, 91, 111–112, 118, 206
Seer, 112
Self, self, 11, 13, 24–27, 29, 36–37, 39, 45–47, 49, 50, 55–56, 63–66, 70, 75, 80, 88–89, 101, 105–107, 112, 118–120, 125, 129, 133, 136–140, 143, 147, 151–152, 163, 170–171, 194, 201, 208–209, 212
Self-actualization, 117, 133, 156, 167, 176, 208
Self esteem, 56
Self image, 48, 50, 91, 134, 167
Self-realization, 23, 40, 51, 65, 91, 111, 118, 121, 140, 170, 176, 208
Senex, 120, 126, 128. See also Puer/senex complex
Separation anxiety, 75
Serpent, 73
Serpent power, 90, 166
Sex magic, 165–166
Sexuality, 57
Shadow, 27, 35–39, 46, 48, 50, 69–70, 103, 127
Shakti, 166
Shaman(ess), 63, 92, 121, 137, 142

Shame, 76
Siddhartha, 120
Siddhas, 143
Silver, 102–103, 183, 191, 193
Sin, 47, 70, 75, 139
Sky, 145, 148–149
Sleep, 186, 190
Social mask, 47. See also Persona
Solificatio, 107, 115, 118
Solutio, 61–70, 133
Solve et coagula, 69–70
Soma, 192
Son, 118, 144, 145, 147, 149, 151,
    159, 161, 165, 172–173, 175, 183,
    185, 198–199, 201
Sophia, 63, 201
Soul, 13–15, 21, 23, 25–26, 30, 39,
    43, 45–46, 49, 53, 63, 77, 82, 89,
    97, 99, 101–102, 104–105, 125–
    126, 134, 140, 145, 155, 159, 164–
    165, 167, 173, 175, 179, 186–187,
    189, 196, 202, 205
Soul guide, 49, 50, 147
Soul-making, 15, 123
Soul mate, 27, 59
Soul-travel, 166
Spirit, 10, 12, 14–15, 21, 25–26, 43,
    45–46, 49, 53, 63, 67, 79, 87–88,
    95, 97, 101–102, 104–105, 112,
    117–118, 120, 123, 125, 141, 145,
    148, 150, 155, 159, 164–165, 173,
    175, 177, 179, 188, 191, 194, 196,
    202, 205
Spiritual development, 109, 111,
    124, 207
Sri Aurobindo, 170
Stag, 42–43, 45, 50
Star of David, 105
Stress, 25, 35, 65, 75
Subconscious, 9, 11, 31, 35, 37, 45,
    49, 55, 64–65, 88, 111, 123, 126,
    134, 136
Sublimatio, 14, 87–92, 133
Sublimation, 48, 73, 85, 91, 98, 118,
    165
Subpersonalities, 48, 56
Subtle body, 102, 103, 111
Suicide, 28, 127
Sulpher, 21,
Sun, 73, 79–80, 87, 103, 107, 118–
    120, 122, 136, 161, 175, 193
Superconscious, 36, 39, 48–49, 51,

56, 90, 136, 163, 176
Superego, 66, 117–118
Sweat, sweating, 173, 177, 182–183,
    185, 191, 193
Swedenborg, 166
Sword, 36, 37
Symbols, 12–13, 24–27, 45, 48–49, 51,
    76, 102–103, 112, 117, 138, 147,
    151, 155, 161, 191, 195
Symptoms, 37, 39, 51
Synchronicity, 4, 134, 138, 209

Talismans, 58
Tantra, 165
Tao, 46, 117, 202
Tarot, 141
Terrible Mother, 77, 78, 82
Therapy, 19, 38, 68, 70, 77, 81, 90,
    97–98, 100, 106, 124–126, 137,
    140, 143, 154, 208
Theresa of Avila, 194
Third eye, 112, 167
Thoth, 87, 180
Throne, 114–115, 117, 145, 199
Time, 78, 136, 203, 207
Tincture, 115, 120, 131, 137, 183,
    185–186, 191, 193
Transcendent function, 11–12, 49,
    161
Transformation, 11, 23–26, 31, 47,
    82, 105, 112, 121, 134, 136, 151,
    208
Transmutation, 13, 23, 133
Traumas, 38, 100, 111, 137
Trickster, 27
Trinity, 17, 180, 193, 201, 207
Trust, 99–100, 164

Ultima materia, 26–27, 151, 211–212
Underworld, 121
Unicorn, 42–43, 45, 50
Unification, 27, 105
Unitive Life, 201–203, 205
Universal consciousness, 27. See also
    Consciousness, cosmic
Universal mind, 169
Universe, 111
Unus Mundus, 97
Urobouros, 75, 78

Values, 30, 35, 45–46, 48, 112, 118, 124
Virgin, 50, 81–82
Virgin Mary, 63, 81
Vishnu, 192
Visualization, 125
Void, 64, 190, 192–193, 209
Von Franz, M. L., 133

Water, 25, 77, 105, 133, 140, 149, 180, 185, 186, 191–193, 199, 206–207
Whale, 121, 189
White, whiteness, whitening, 33, 43, 61, 64, 94–95, 97–98, 101, 103–104
White Goddess, 81
Wholeness, 26, 37, 39, 45, 50, 67, 76, 79, 105, 118–119, 122, 136, 137, 140, 151, 169–171, 193
Whore of Babylon, 78
Will, 106, 117–118, 133, 135–137, 145, 176, 192, 204
Wisdom, 16–18, 53, 63–64, 91, 101, 106, 118, 136, 140–141, 165, 167, 169, 171
Wise Old Man, 27, 68, 81, 85, 91, 119, 141, 149, 162–163
Wise Old Woman, 68, 82
Wizard, 48, 63, 124
Wolf, 60–61, 64, 66–68
Woodman, Marion, 122
Worldview, 68, 98, 133–134, 137, 201
Wounded Healer, 97, 137, 142

Yellow, 103, 138
Yin and yang, 46, 166
Yoga, 105, 125, 143, 202–203
Yoni, 166
Yuppie lifestyle, 31

Zaddik, 211

THE ALCHEMICAL ENGRAVINGS
OF LAMBSPRINCK

A Limited Edition Portfolio of One Thousand Copies

OAK Publishing
2005

If you have enjoyed Joel Radcliffe's pen and ink renderings reproduced in *The Modern Alchemist*, you might be interested to learn about the limited edition art portfolio of "The Alchemical Engravings of Lambsprinck" published in connection with this book.

Issued in a limited edition of one thousand copies, the portfolio contains larger reproductions of all sixteen engravings, printed on permanent, acid-free paper. The prints are collected together in a special envelope that features Lambsprinck's Coat of Arms reproduced on the front. The illustrations are suitable for framing and will be sent in a sturdy cardboard mailer.

To order a copy of the limited edition portfolio,
Send a check or money order for $15.00
plus $5.00 Shipping to:

OAK Publishing
Attn: Richard Miller
1212 S.W. 5th St.
Grants Pass, OR 97526